Cats: Their Health and Care

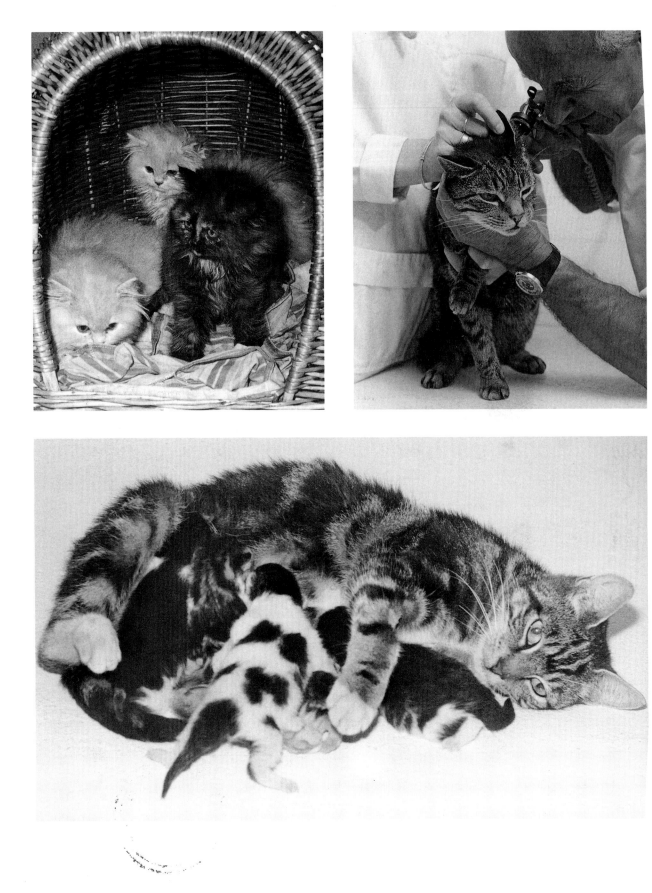

Cats
Their Health and Care

Eddie Straiton

FARMING PRESS

First published 1977
Second edition 1991

ISBN 0 85236 218 8

A catalogue record for this book is available
from the British Library

Published by Farming Press Books
4 Friars Courtyard, 30-32 Princes Street
Ipswich IP1 1RJ, United Kingdom

Distributed in North America
by Diamond Farm Enterprises,
Box 537, Alexandria Bay, NY 13607, USA

Cover design by Andrew Thistlethwaite
Phototypeset by Typestylers, Ipswich
Printed and bound in Great Britain by Butler and Tanner, Frome, Somerset

Contents

BREEDING

HEALTH, DISEASE AND GENERAL CONDITIONS

A colour section appears between pages 52 and 53

Preface

The damp Scotch mist soaked through my threadbare sailor's jersey as I stood shivering at the corner of Sloan Avenue, one of Scotland's most disreputable streets in the industrially depressed town of Clydebank. It was 4 a.m. on the morning after my eighth birthday. The year, 1925, and I was just about to start my first job, delivering milk with Jock the milkman for the princely weekly wage of threepence.

My bare feet beat a tattoo on the pavement in an effort to keep warm and the ice-cold gusts of wet wind searched silently but rudely under my short kilt.

Suddenly I felt an exquisite warmth against a calf muscle and heard clearly in the morning quiet the soft murmuring tremors of happiness — it was Blackie — *my* cat, purring his head off with goodwill. I picked him up and hugged him as he spoke to me — three short sharp meows of

comradeship and encouragement.

Since that memorable moment I have never been without a cat, and over the years have built up a tremendous love and respect for the feline species. I admire especially their courage, agility and resolute independence.

This book has been created in an effort to help cat owners throughout the world by providing in simple non-technical language a reference book which will benefit both them and their pets.

I would like to thank my secretary and staff for their patience and help, and also my photographers, Tony Boydon and Godfrey Sittig; artist Richard Perry; and also my wife Penny, who produced some of the latest colour photographs.

Eddie Straiton

DEDICATION

To the memory of my colleague and friend

ALAN L. L. McKERRELL

*whose character and skill inspired
all who knew him and whose courage and
manly dignity epitomised the essential
masculinity of the veterinary profession.
Tough but sensitive, Alan had a
heart of gold and an incredible kindliness
towards all God's creatures.*

Cats: Their Health and Care

Know Your Cat

I

The Cat's Anatomy

Cats have an amazingly supple bony framework which gives them an uncanny litheness (*diagram A*).

The skeleton, comprising approximately 234 bones, is remarkably pliable. The hind legs can produce a leap of up to six feet or more; the forelegs can apparently twist in any direction; the head can be swivelled round rapidly and fully either way; and the spine has a mobility far greater than in any other domestic animal. One only has to watch the snaking movements of the cat's tail to fully appreciate the tractility of its vertebrae.

A cat's bones are very similar to those of humans (including two collar bones). They are linked together by approximately the same number of muscles as our own, that is, over 500, but many of the cat's muscles are more powerfully developed than in humans, especially in the hind quarters and neck (*diagram B*). Hence the cat's powerful spring and its ability to strike rapidly and decisively at its prey.

The cat has a comparatively small chest, with the contents — the heart and lungs — correspondingly reduced in size. Because of this it tires more easily than a dog, exhibiting bursts of terrific energy followed by long periods of rest.

The abdomen, however, is roomy enough to allow for gorging and fasting as most carnivores have to do in the wild state.

Diagram A

ANATOMY OF THE CAT

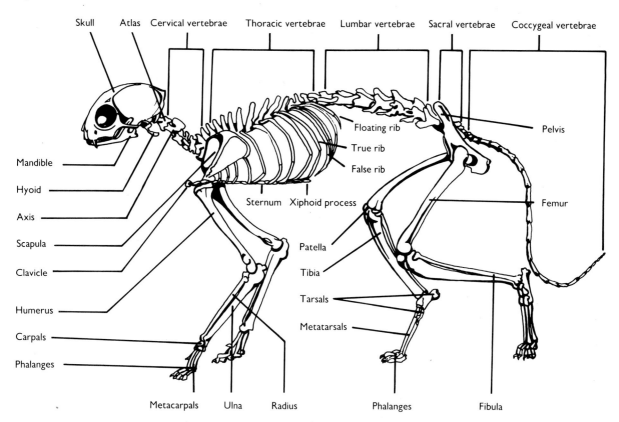

Skull   Atlas   Cervical vertebrae   Thoracic vertebrae   Lumbar vertebrae   Sacral vertebrae   Coccygeal vertebrae

Floating rib

True rib

False rib

Pelvis

Mandible

Hyoid

Axis

Scapula

Clavicle

Humerus

Carpals

Phalanges

Sternum   Xiphoid process

Femur

Patella

Tibia

Tarsals

Metatarsals

Metacarpals   Ulna   Radius   Phalanges   Fibula

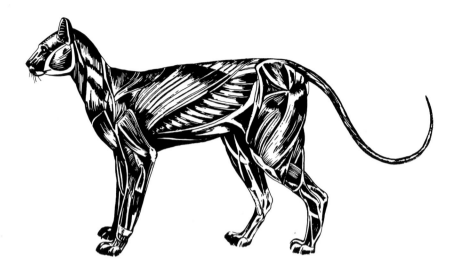

2
The Cat's Physiology

A well-developed brain co-ordinating muscle balance and direction gives the cat lightning reactions — vital necessities for its success as a predator (*photo 1*).

The cat walks on its toes, five on each front foot and four on each hind. The fleshy pads have a downy covering and this, together with tufts of fur between the pads, allows stealth in stalking prey. At the same time, the paws have an acute sensitivity. The cat uses its front paws in much the same way as we use our hands — holding and lifting food and objects, testing temperature, swatting and fondling, and so on. The hind paws are bigger and stronger, giving tremendous propulsion for jumping and running.

The claws (*photo 2*) come into play during fighting and scratching; they also provide powerful extra grip on any surface as seen when the cat is climbing a tree.

In young kittens the claws are not retractile, but usually after three or four months they can be withdrawn though the withdrawal is not complete in some cats, Siamese especially. If the cat is kept

1

2

mostly indoors the claws will require regular clipping.

The tail (*photo 3*) assists in balance, but perhaps in the domestic cat its main physiological function is as an indication of mood. When the tip twitches there is anticipation of something new and exciting; a furious lashing of the whole tail denotes anger — a gentle waving, pleasure. A sudden jerk often means indignation or surprise.

Perhaps the most important part of a cat's sensory apparatus is its whiskers (*photo 4 and colour plate 1*) — they not only aid the cat's sight but in the dark help to replace it. Many people think the whiskers can pick out objects by slight changes in the air pressure around them.

The eyebrows have a similar action, as do groups of tactile hairs found one on each foreleg at the back of the wrist. In fact the entire body of the cat is hypersensitive to the touch, especially behind the ears and down the spine.

The coat or fur comprises four different types of hair, except for Rex-coated cats which boast only one or two. In cold weather the coat thickens and is oiled by a sebaceous secretion which produces the exquisite sheen of the healthy cat (*photo 5*).

3

4

5

The sebaceous glands are not sweat glands: the only sweat glands similar to ours are found between the pads of the paws.

A healthy cat is scrupulously clean and rarely smells unpleasant, even less so when neutered. It washes and grooms itself with its rough tongue (*photo 6*) which acts like a curry comb and dandy brush at one and the same time. The roughness on the tongue is due to extremely powerful papillae coarse enough to rasp a bone smooth (*photo 7 and colour plate 2*). Unfortunately the papillae slope backwards and this means that anything that gets lodged on them has to be swallowed. This explains why cats often swallow sharp-pointed objects like needles.

The tongue is also used as a spoon when the cat is lapping or drinking (*photo 8*).

6

7
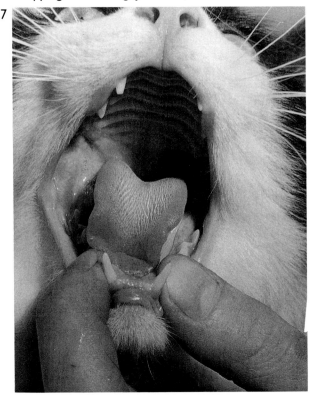

8

4

3
The Cat's Natural Instincts

The cat's natural instincts are hyper-acute, especially the homing instinct.

I did not fully appreciate just how strong this was until I had a case of a cat travelling 40 or more miles over foreign territory, and through two strange towns, to return home in less than sixteen hours.

I found this remarkable, but there is an authentic American story of a cat finding its way across more than 2,000 miles of continent to reach its owner's new home, which it had never seen before — quite incredible, especially since the journey took five months.

Some people are convinced that the cat can distinguish spiritual presence. Certainly I've seen a cat bristle up for no apparent reason and follow with its eyes some invisible object or person across a room.

Most cats appear to have an instinctive time sense. They seem to know which day of the week it is and can clock to a second their feeding time (*photo 1*). I've seen this on many occasions with my hospital cats. Neutered cats who enjoy the warmth of a home will always return to the house before locking-up time.

There is ample evidence that feline instinct provides a premonition of danger and an awareness of crisis or death in a household. Certainly cats may well have a sixth sense denied to us humans.

Nonetheless it is the pleasurable duty of every cat owner to learn as much as possible about his or her pet, and I can assure you the cat provides a fascinating study.

Without doubt one of the most intelligent of all animals, the cat hunts like an Indian, moving in short bursts with its body close to the ground. It freezes at the slightest sound or hint of danger, manoeuvres patiently into position on the leeward side of its quarry and then pounces like lightning, grabbing its prey with claws and teeth simultaneously.

Contrary to general belief, cats develop great affection for their owners though they are not so demonstrative as dogs. Not only so, but their

character is greatly affected by their human environment. For example, a neurotic cat often has a neurotic owner and an affectionate cat invariably has a happy home.

The cat is very possessive of what it regards as its 'territory' — usually the back garden. It marks the boundaries by spraying urine and will often attack any stray who dares encroach.

The pattern of behaviour is also extremely interesting. When annoyed or scared it will bristle up with the fur literally standing on end; at the same time the tail bushes out like a spreading tree and fans slowly from side to side (*photo 2*).

If facing up to a dog it will arch its back, stare defiantly at the foe and hiss or spit. When the dog gets too near, one or other of the paws with the rapier-like claws fully extended flashes out like lightning. Such courage is incredible. I've seen one cat keeping three dogs at bay until one by one the canine aggressors have sneaked off each with a badly lacerated face and its tail between its legs.

By the same token, if confronted by its owner in the act of wrong-doing, a cat behaves rather like a child being scolded, dragging its tail and dropping its head apologetically or running off somewhere to hide. If, however, it considers that it is in the right it will loudly protest innocence — in such cases, with my own cats I can imagine them cursing me!

Just one last instinct which I think makes the cat the ideal household pet — an instinct for tidiness as well as cleanliness. I've seen my own cats visibly protesting when I've fed them on a plate containing the remnants of their previous night's feed!

4
The Cat's Senses

The Ears

(Sense of Sound)
The cat's hearing has a range twice as great as that of humans.

The large ears trap and concentrate the sound, and since they are extremely mobile and flexible, their efficiency is almost incredible (*photo 1*). Cats have been known to distinguish between two similar sounds less than a yard apart at 60 to 70 feet.

This super hearing is manifest in a cat's general behaviour. For instance, often my own cat will leap out virtually from nowhere as soon as I start sharpening the knife to cut up his supper or open the fridge door to take out the milk.

The inner ear is similar in structure to the human one, though the balance mechanism must be more efficient than ours because rarely do cats suffer from travel sickness.

Blue-eyed white cats nearly always exhibit congenital deafness, but their sense of balance or equilibrium is seldom impaired.

The Voice

(Sense of Speech or Communication)
There can be little doubt that cats have a language all their own. One only has to listen to be convinced of this.

When angry they growl, snarl, spit and screech.

When courting the tom often croons softly to his lady love.

The mother cat speaks to her kittens in a language never used by other cats — soft murmurs and subdued squeaks or meows (*photo 2*).

The domestic cat communicates with its owner again and again in the same language with different distinct squeaks or meows for begging, greeting or requesting and unmistakable cursing when frustrated or angry.

Purring, of course, occurs only in cats and its specific cause is not yet fully understood. It seems

1

2

to be mainly a sign of happiness or contentment, though it can occur when the cat is scared or in pain.

When a sleeping cat starts purring, it may well be having a pleasant dream.

My purely personal opinion is that the noise emanates chiefly from completely relaxed vocal cords, and similar noise is produced when the same cords are tensed up by pain or fear. One thing is certain: purring is rarely if ever heard when a cat is seriously ill.

The Eyes
(Sense of Sight)

The cat's eyes are much more efficient than those of a human. Comparatively larger, they can focus and adjust the pupil in a fraction of a second and judge distances almost instantaneously (*photo 3*).

The pupil, which controls the light entry, enlarges from a narrow slit to a full circle and contracts just as swiftly.

Since many of them hunt at night, cats can be described as nocturnal. Probably because of this they possess a triangular layer of reflecting cells in the upper half of the eye to reflect light, which has already passed through the eye, back on to the retinal cells. This allows cats to apparently see in the dark, although in fact they require at least some dim light. Certainly they use their sight rather than scent to spot danger and to locate their prey.

The eyes are well forward in the head and this allows overlapping fields of vision giving each eye a field or angle of vision of more than 200°.

Contrary to folk lore, cats are not colour blind, though their colour apparatus is not so well developed as in humans.

Rising from the inner corner of each eye is a third eyelid, called the nictitating membrane (*photo 4*). This is of great value to the cat, protecting the eye in many circumstances, e.g. during a fight, when prowling through long grass, etc. It also acts as a filter against very strong light and helps to clean the eye.

Over the years I have found the third eyelid a useful guide in clinical practice. When the cat is off-colour, the nictitating membranes come across the eyes and remain partially closed. They do the same thing when the cat is heavily infested with worms, though a bellyful of grasshoppers can also produce the identical syndrome. In some breeds I have

noticed that the third eyelid is always visible, but the majority of healthy cats rarely show it.

3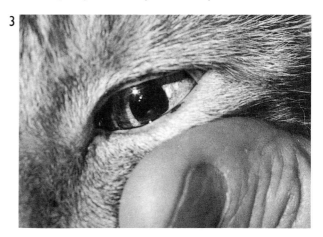

4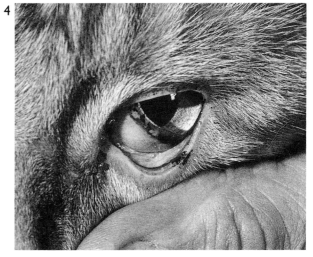

The Nostrils
(Sense of Scent)

The feline scent or sense of smell is well developed and very important; although not used primarily in hunting (as with dogs), it appears to be vital in the location of food at close quarters. Often I have seen a cat staring straight at a piece of meat but only identifying it after a good sniff all around. This instinct may stem from the fact that for the first few days of life a kitten relies on scent to find the mother's nipples and to start sucking. Certainly it is not because the cat is long-sighted.

Without doubt smell plays a big part in sexual identification. Nothing smells worse than the urine of an uncastrated adult tom, and entire queens emit a characteristic odour especially when in season. Neutered cats lack these sex odours and this is probably the main reason why entire cats tend to attack them.

However, all cats neutered or otherwise enjoy investigating scents, especially on each other's coats. Many are fascinated by certain plants, especially catmint, and all seem to relish the powerful perfumes of women.

To sum up, therefore, the cat's sense of smell is acutely developed but is not used primarily in hunting. In this respect the cat is identical to monkeys and humans.

The Mouth
(Sense of Taste)

This is not particularly well developed in the cat, though distinctive taste buds are present on the tongue and a few smaller ones exist in the soft palate and mouth lining (*photo 5*).

Certainly the cat is able to discern its favourite flavours.

5

5
Choosing a Cat as a Pet

In the main, cats require less attention than any other pet, especially the short-coated ones. They are clean, tough, lively and independent.

When you add to that the many other facets of its personality, the cat bids fair to be the perfect domestic pet.

Nonetheless it requires regular and correct feeding and if long haired, regular daily brushing and combing (*photo 1*).

If you live in the country or have a garden, then the cat will happily settle down on its own.

If you live in a flat, then it will probably need a mate to prevent boredom ruining its life.

If you are a nervous person, choose a cat with a placid temperament like a silver tabby.

If your job or life involves repeated removals, then one of the exotic cats like the Siamese (*photo 2*) is probably best since it seems to dislike environmental changes less than other breeds.

If you do not intend to breed from your pet

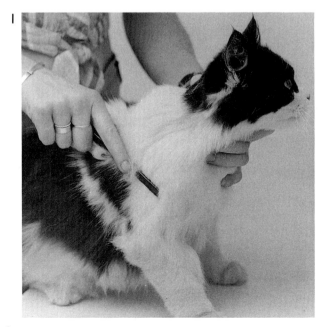

1

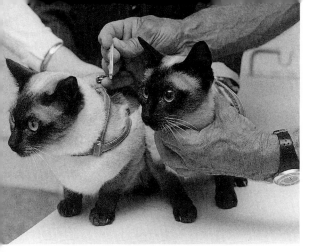

have it neutered and vaccinated against enteritis at the earliest possible moment. Twelve weeks is the minimal age (*photo 3*). Personally I advise vaccination at 12 weeks and neutering at six months. Whatever happens, never allow a male pet to reach sexual maturity. If you do, your house and outbuildings will perpetually reek of tom cat odour. If the female is allowed to go beyond the six-month mark, you may well find yourself with a houseful of kittens.

If and when your cats are neutered, careful feeding is necessary to avoid obesity (see Feeding, pages 11-13).

Just one last point — if you have small children, then make sure your first cat is at least six months old and able to take care of itself. Small kittens, though lovable and playful, can be and often are seriously injured when awkwardly grabbed or dropped.

Cats as pets for older people
Considerable medical research has shown that pets not only provide companionship for older people but can prolong their lives. In my opinion and that of many doctors, the cat is the ideal pet. It is loyal, friendly and easy to care for. Unlike a dog it does not demand controlled exercise and it is a constant source of comfort, especially to old people living alone.

As one of the higher animals a cat can survive in the wild and this instinct ensures that the domestic cat looks after itself to a large degree. Nonetheless, for a happy and long liaison the golden rules to follow are:

Have the cat neutered and regularly vaccinated against the killer disease feline enteritis.

Groom the coat at least once a day, preferably twice with long-haired cats.

If the cat has to spend most of its time indoors, provide a litter tray, which should be emptied and cleaned daily.

Feed in the same place and at regular times, always using clean dishes since the cat is fastidious and a naturally clean animal. Fresh, clean drinking water should always be available. Milk is not essential.

Provide a warm, comfortable bed, lined preferably with newspapers which can be renewed daily.

Get your veterinary surgeon to inject or treat the cat for worms as or when necessary. If the cat is a hunter, it will require dosing every six months.

6
Handling a Cat

The best way to pick up an adult cat, especially when it is pregnant, is by grasping the scruff of the neck with one hand and placing the other hand simultaneously under the backside (*photo 1*). With this hold, the cat's full weight is not on the scruff and the cat feels comfortable.

With a kitten, put one hand underneath it and cradle the whole body in the palm, with the other hand under the neck to support the head (*photo 2*).

The ideal method of carrying a cat is in the crook of the arm with the opposite hand caressing its neck.

The best grip for restraining the cat is by the scruff of the neck (*photo 3*).

To control its paws, sit the cat in the crook of one arm holding its rear paws with that hand while you grip the front paws with the other.

If, however, the cat is strange or wild, such a hold invites a very painful bite on the hand. When handling a strange cat, therefore, it is wisest to have someone hold the scruff of the neck firmly while you hold the paws (*photo 4*).

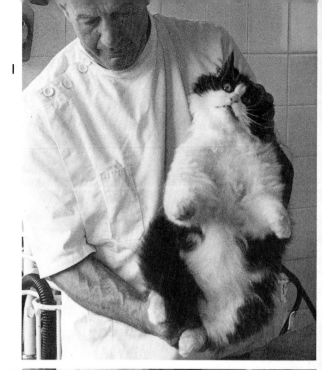

When holding the cat for a veterinary surgeon to inject it, a good tip is to hold the scruff of the neck with one hand and press firmly downwards on the cat's back with the other. When dosing it with liquid medicine or attempting to give it a tablet, it is wise to get an assistant to wrap the cat tightly in a large towel, leaving only the head protruding.

After any type of surgery it is best not to handle the cat for at least ten days. This simple precaution not only aids the healing of the wound and prevents the bursting of stitches, but just as important it avoids pain to the animal: an inevitable result of any stretching of the operation area.

Handling during transportation

The golden rule is to travel as little as possible — most cats hate it.

Although many adult domestic cats appear to almost enjoy travelling loose in a car, it is always

best to use an escape-proof basket. Apart from the fact that the cat may shoot off through an open window, it may distract the driver's attention and cause an accident.

On a long journey a well-ventilated cat box

5 the sedative half an hour before the journey; the effect will last up to seven hours (*photo 6 and colour plate 3*). The injection is preferable to oral tablets not only because it works much quicker but because it is much easier to give. With the odd cat that is prone to car sickness, withhold food for eight hours before the journey and liquids for at least three hours.

If the cat is unaccompanied, it is best to have it injected with a heavy dose of tranquilliser which will ensure sleep for most of the way. At the same time, provide a larger travelling box containing a litter tray or at least a sawdust area for the inevitable toilet requirements.

6
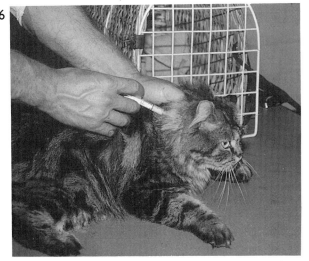

similar to the one illustrated is ideal (*photo 5*). A collar and lead are an advantage since the trained cat will require the opportunities to empty itself.

I am often asked if a cat should be sedated before a long journey. Obviously this depends on the pet's temperament. As a rule it is not necessary. If, however, the cat is excitable, it is advisable to get your veterinary surgeon to inject

General Care of the Cat

7
Feeding

Feeding is the most important item in the life of a domestic cat. Cats are carnivores — i.e. meat-eating animals. In the natural state they would live on raw, freshly killed meat and bones plus the vegetable matter contained in the stomachs of their prey.

With this constantly in mind, therefore, correct feeding presents no problems.

Any form of meat — red or white — is suitable, raw or partially cooked, chopped up fine together with fragments of raw or partially cooked green vegetables, lettuce, carrot, etc. (*photo 1*). The meat provides protein, and the vegetables supply the minerals and vitamins, especially the important vitamin A which a cat cannot synthesise. The diet can be balanced with bread or cereals to provide carbohydrates, but these should never form the major portion of the feed.

Alternate sources of protein are fish, cheese and eggs with occasional tinned sardines and pilchards which are ideal as laxative feeds.

Liver should only be given occasionally — say once a week. When fed raw it is a laxative; cooked it may cause constipation.

Spleen can also cause diarrhoea and should be fed no more than twice a week.

Lungs (or lights) are safe and nourishing but should be cut up into small pieces, using sharp scissors, or better still put through a mincer.

Milk is not an essential part of a cat's diet as so many people think; in fact some cats can't digest cow's milk properly. It is always advisable, therefore, to offer your cat both water and milk (*photo 2*). It will very soon show you which it prefers, and in any case, every cat needs clean drinking water no matter how much milk he may imbibe.

Cats eat fresh growing grass as a source of vitamins and roughage (*photo 3*). The grass often makes the cat vomit and helps to bring up fur balls.

There are a wide variety of cat foods on the market. It has been my experience that *dry* feeding predisposes to bladder deposits and urinary retention often with fatal results. Canned meat and

2

1

3

fish products are therefore preferable since they contain a large percentage of water, and most of them also have added minerals and vitamins. However, if feeding them exclusively, it is wise to add vitamin B to the diet in the form of yeast or Marmite since some canned foods are deficient in this vitamin.

A large raw bone for the cat to chew at will provide all the calcium and phosphorus needed (*photo 4*).

4

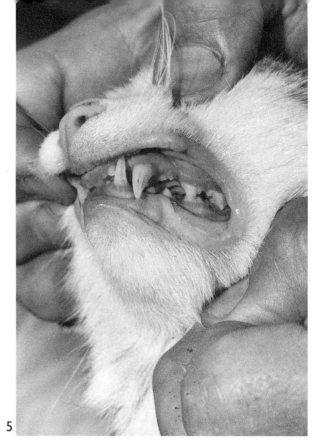

5

And now the daily ration. I am repeatedly asked what quantity an adult cat should be fed. The correct balanced diet is half-an-ounce per pound body weight (25 g per kg) fed once daily; for example, an average 10 lb (4.5 kg) cat requires 5 oz (113 g) daily plus ad lib clean, fresh drinking water. This may not seem very much but it is sufficient to keep the cat fit and healthy. Many cats will eat three or four times this amount, but if they do so continually and especially if they have been neutered, they will grow excessively fat and lazy.

If in doubt at any time, consult your veterinary surgeon.

As a cat is a hunter and a carcase-eating animal, its teeth and digestive system are designed to deal with meat and the other edible parts of a carcase — soft bones, stomach contents, etc.

The teeth are adapted for killing and tearing — not chewing (*photo 5 and colour plate 4*). The razor sharp 'fangs' or incisor teeth are deadly to its prey — mice, rats, birds, reptiles and other mammals.

All cats enjoy catching and eating flies and insects, especially grasshoppers. Although I've treated many a cat that has made itself sick by eating too many grasshoppers, the odd grasshopper is a delicacy and the flies appear to do no harm.

Fish is another favourite food and many cats have trained themselves to catch fish, scooping the unsuspecting creatures out of ponds with their paws.

8
House Training

Kittens are naturally clean animals and the majority will have been taught by mother where to go — be it a litter box (*photo 1*) or selected spots in the garden.

If the mother has always used a litter box, then during the training of the kitten make sure that the box is cleaned and filled with fresh litter at least twice a day. If the litter becomes excessively

soiled, the kitten's natural instinct for cleanliness may prompt it to go elsewhere.

If the odd accident occurs and you see it happening, don't knock the kitten about or 'rub his nose in it' — chastise him firmly and carry him to the tray. He'll learn quickly.

As the kitten grows, move the litter tray outside the door, then onto the earth in a corner of the garden. After a week or two in this site the tray can be dispensed with.

Persistent offenders

I occasionally meet owners who swear they can't train their kitten no matter what they do.

The simple reason for failure is a lack of hygiene in the kitten's patrol area. If a misplaced urine patch or mess is not cleaned up thoroughly, then the persistent odour will make the kitten return to the same spot.

I always advise an immediate thorough clean-up followed by a soaking with a powerful deodorant (*photo 2*). When this is done the kitten will not use that spot again.

2

9
Housing

A cat may be housed indoors or in an outbuilding. The ideal is the best of both worlds — free access to the exciting outside world plus the warm refuge of its comfortable bed.

If circumstances demand that the cat remains housebound (for instance, in a flat or a home in a busy town with no garden) then keep two cats for companionship, especially if the house is left empty during the day.

To obtain the ideal, it is advisable to fit a special cat door to the shelter your pet regards as his own, be it a kitchen or an insulated outhouse (*photo 1 and colour plate 5*).

The cat door is merely a small flap, hinged and weighted, which the cat can push open either way. The weight automatically keeps the flap closed and protects from draught.

It's not a bad idea to fit a bolt to the flap in case you wish to keep the cat in, e.g. when it is ill or when an unspayed queen is in season.

The adult cat will soon choose its favourite

1

14

sleeping spot. All you need to provide is a warm basket with a half-curved back to protect the cat's back (*photo 2*); a home-made wooden box will serve just as well.

The best bedding of all is newspaper. Apart from the fact that it is probably the warmest of all available materials (tramps sleeping out in the winter use newspapers as blankets), it's the cheapest and the most hygienic.

A clean bed can be provided at least once daily, and at the same time the soiled newspapers can be burned or put in the dustbin. In this way any 'strangers' (fleas, lice, etc.) from the cat will be seen and destroyed and appropriate control action can be set in motion (see External Parasites, page 40).

The young, newly acquired kitten

It is with the young, newly acquired kitten that commonsense and housing facilities are most important.

The essentials (*photo 3*) are:
    A litter box
    Feeding and drinking bowls
    A warm bed
The 'extras' are:
    A collar or harness with an identity tag in
    case your new friend runs off before getting
    to know its new quarters
    A travelling basket

2

Litter box

I always think this is wrongly named since a metal tray with raised edges (like a baking tin) is preferable. This provides more space and is much easier to clean than a wooden box. However, specially made plastic trays are probably the ideal.

The best litter? A mixture of sawdust and peat moss, though the various proprietary brands available are also very satisfactory (*photo 4*). Newspaper is not suitable as a litter, though a thick layer *under* the litter makes the job of cleaning the tray much easier.

The litter should be changed every day and the tray washed thoroughly with a non-irritant

4

A collar or harness
My advice here is to fit these at the earliest possible age; otherwise the kittens may resent them and do everything to get them off. The ideal collar should have an expandable elastic section in case the cat gets hung up during its prowling (*photo 6*). Personally I prefer the harness; it is safer than a collar and much better if the cat has to

6

detergent and rinsed well. Whatever you do, never use a strong-smelling soap or antiseptic; if you do, the kitten won't use the tray. And remember: some soaps and disinfectants are poisonous to cats.

Feeding and drinking bowls
Both should be solid and stable with a weighted bottom and a narrow rim (*photo 5*). Saucers are

be walked on a lead. Probably the real advantage of the collar or harness is that it allows the wearing of an identity tag — very important during the kitten's settling-down period. Later, in the interest of the cat's safety, it is best dispensed with.

Travelling basket
This is a worthwhile extra if only for taking the kitten to your veterinary surgeon. Again and again I've seen owners seriously scratched in their efforts to transport their cats loose in a car.

The ideal cat basket should be at least 1 ft wide, 1½ ft long and 1 ft high (305 mm × 455 mm × 305 mm) (*colour plate 6*). Personally I prefer solid baskets like the one illustrated (*photo 7*) — I've seen too many cats escape from cardboard and wicker baskets. The solid types are also much easier to clean.

5

not ideal since they are easily tipped over if or when the hungry kitten steps on the edge.

Many cats pull the food from the bowls, so it's a good idea to set the bowls on a generous square of newspaper.

A warm bed
As with the adult, I've found that the kitten takes to the half-curved basket quicker than any other manufactured bed, though some kittens select their own sleeping spot, often on top of a kitchen cupboard. Wherever the kitten settles, provide a clean bed of newspapers every day.

7

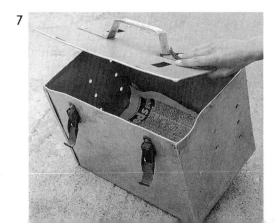

10
Introducing a Cat to its New Home

When you take the cat out of the basket in the new surroundings, stroke it gently and talk quietly. Introduce it to the litter tray and offer some food, milk or water, but keep the door shut. Kittens will take to new surroundings quicker than adult cats, but nevertheless they all require a settling period and during that time it is important to block up escape avenues **for at least three days** (*colour plate 7*).

The first sign that the new pet is feeling safe in its new environment is when it starts to wash itself (*photo 1*). Incidentally, if you acquire an adult tom, make sure you have it neutered at least a month before you give it access to your home; otherwise the unpleasant smell from the litter tray will filter through the entire household.

If you already have a cat or dog give the newcomer at least a day to settle before you introduce them. It is surprising how quickly they will accept each other. Don't panic if the initial reaction appears violent: within a few hours natural curiosity plus an instinctive desire for companionship will sort things out, especially if, in the beginning at least, you make a great fuss of the resident and ignore the newcomer. Jealousy is just as dangerous in animals as it is in humans.

I

11
Grooming

As I have already said, healthy cats are scrupulously clean and will spend hours every day washing themselves. Their rough tongue surface is better than any comb or brush and reaches all parts of the body except the head, shoulders and back of the neck; these areas are cleaned by the cat's paws.

Healthy, short-haired cats therefore do not require grooming unless they become caked in mud. Nonetheless, with housed cats it is a good idea to comb them once daily as an insurance against hairs on the furniture.

Long-haired cats, however, require a lot of attention. They should be combed and brushed twice daily to prevent matting of the fur (*colour plate 8*). Again and again I see neglected long-haired

cats which require anaesthesia and several hours with scissors and clippers to remove tufts of matted hair (*photo 1*). If you start with regular grooming when you have the kitten, he will soon accept and enjoy this attention.

Metal combs (wide-toothed and fine-toothed) and nylon brushes are best (*photo 2*).

During the grooming inspect the ears, the paws and the claws. If the ears appear dirty, the hair tufted between the paws or the claws too long, then consult your veterinary surgeon at once.

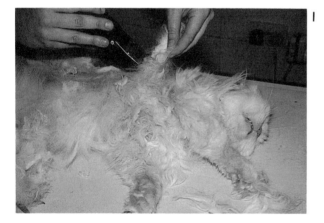

12

Bathing and Moulting

Bathing
Bathing a cat is indicated only in exceptional circumstances, for example, in parasitic conditions or when the coat gets covered in any substance dangerous for the cat to lick.

The job is not easy and is best left to a veterinary surgeon or a trained veterinary nurse (*photo 1*). Certainly never attempt to bath a cat without at least veterinary advice.

Moulting

Kittens have their first moult at a year old irrespective of season. Thereafter, if they are domestic, they will moult all the year round but especially in the summer and early autumn.

Wild cats moult at one year and thereafter only in summer and autumn.

1

13
General Signs of Ill Health

It is important to notice when your cat is off-colour so that you can take it to the veterinary surgeon at the earliest possible moment.

The first sign of sickness in all animals is loss of appetite — if your cat refuses its normal feed then get it to your vet quickly.

Vomiting? A single vomit, especially in the summertime when the cat is eating grass, grasshoppers and birds, should give no cause for worry, but if the vomiting persists attention is required.

Diarrhoea in any cat, especially one that has not been vaccinated against feline enteritis, demands immediate veterinary attention.

Sneezing and/or running eyes denote an early stage flu virus which responds rapidly to veterinary treatment.

Crouching over the drinking bowl, as though wanting to drink but unable to do so, is a sign of another virus which attacks the tonsils and pharynx and which again must be treated quickly by your veterinary surgeon (*photo 1*).

Head shaking, ear scratching, or holding the head awkwardly indicates ear trouble — again a job for the veterinary surgeon.

Bad breath and dribbling from the mouth probably mean that the teeth require attention (*photo 2 and colour plate 9*).

1

2

Repeated straining to urinate or defaecate suggest bladder or bowel trouble, both of which must be treated promptly.

Persistent coat scratching and bald patches may be due to fleas, lice, mange, ringworm or hormonal eczemas, all of which require the skill and knowledge of a veterinary surgeon to cure.

The cat's temperature is taken by inserting a thermometer into the cat's rectum and this is best done by a veterinary surgeon. The normal temperature is 101.5°F (38.5°C).

To sum up: If your cat is off-colour for any more than a maximum of twenty-four hours, get it to the veterinary surgeon immediately.

14
Nursing and Bandaging

The instinct of a sick cat is to hide and suffer silently, but commonsense nursing can help greatly in its recovery.

A show of restrained affection and concern without persistent fuss, plus a comfortable bed in the cat's chosen refuge, and frequently changed cold drinking water, can work wonders.

Once daily take over the toilet duties with a comb and brush but do them as quickly as possible.

Bathe the eyes (*photo 1*) and nostrils in normal saline solution (one teaspoonful of salt to a pint of water or two teaspoonfuls to the litre) and if the nostrils are cracked, smear them with vaseline or cod-liver oil.

Carry the seriously ill patient onto the lawn several times daily and support it during is efforts. If the rear end is soiled, wash it gently with warm water and detergent and dry thoroughly.

Fortunately, bandaging a cat nowadays is rarely if ever required. In fact, sulphonamides and long-acting antibiotics have virtually eliminated the necessity, except in the case of simple fractures where plaster bandages are still used (*photo 2*). Certainly, if you think any form of bandage is needed, consult your veterinary surgeon; any attempt by an owner to bandage a cat is rarely successful.

1

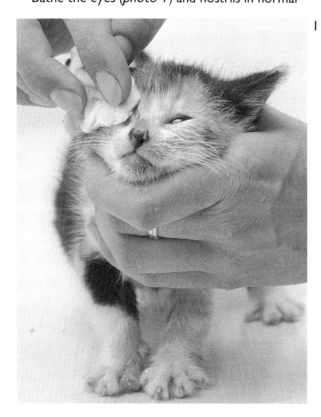

2

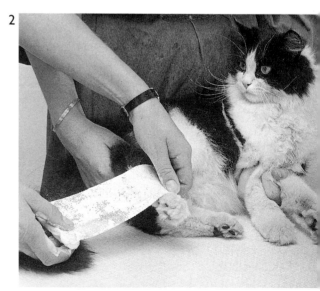

15
Giving Medicines

The easiest method of giving medicines, apart from injections, is to medicate the drinking water or milk. If, however, the patient is too ill to drink, then liquid medicine or pills may be needed.

The safest and best way to give liquid medicine is by using a plastic syringe (*photo 1*). Stand the cat on a table or on the draining board at the side of the sink; grab the scruff of the neck and hold the cat's head back, pouch out the loose skin at the corner of the mouth and squirt the medicine in very slowly. To make the cat swallow, pinch the nostrils. With a nervous cat, get an assistant to wrap all four legs firmly in a large towel. See Chapter 6, Handling a Cat.

To administer a pill rapidly and effectively you need an assistant to stop the cat moving backwards by holding the scruff of the neck with one hand and both forelegs firmly with the other hand.

Put the palm of the left hand across the top of the head and with the thumb and fingers force the cat's mouth wide open. Pop the tablet as far back on the tongue as possible (*photo 2*), and with a rapid movement of the right forefinger, poke it into the back of the throat, then close the cat's mouth sharply. In ninety-nine cases out of a hundred the tablet or pill will be swallowed immediately.

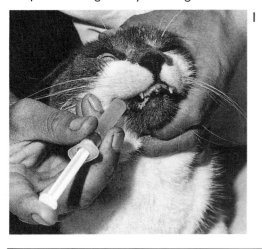

1

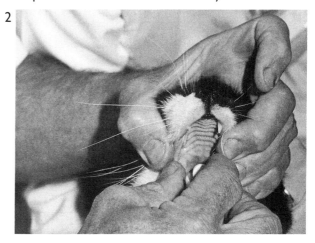

2

Breeding
16
Birth Control

The three forms of birth control are:
1. Castration of the male
2. Spaying of the female
3. Contraceptive injections and pills

If you do not intend to breed with your pet, then castration or spaying by a veterinary surgeon is a must.

The best age?
Opinions differ but personally I prefer to operate when the kittens are six months old. At that age neither the male nor female is sexually mature and both are strong enough to withstand even prolonged anaesthesia.

The best anaesthetic?
I prefer open mask fluothane or halothane — both extremely safe, but there are other very satisfactory short-acting anaesthetics, especially a drug called Saffan which is given intravenously.

Castration
This presents no problems, and provided the job is done professionally using strict asepsis and precautionary antibiotic dressings, there are not likely to be any complications (*plate 1*).

Spaying
Spaying is a simple but highly skilled operation involving opening up the cat's abdomen and removing the ovaries or the entire reproductive tract. Personally I prefer and always practise the latter.

Contraceptive injections and pills
These are not entirely satisfactory in cats and certainly should not be used continuously, but your veterinary surgeon will advise on individual cases. One possible sequel to their persistent use is uterine infection.

17
Sexuality

The male cat reaches puberty (sexual maturity) at around one year old, with a variability of about two months either way. It remains sexually active for the whole of its life unless it is castrated.

The female becomes mature about the same age but is sexually interested only when in season. Generally speaking, the mating periods occur every three or four weeks, chiefly in the spring and summer, but there are no hard or fast rules, especially with some of the more exotic breeds. Certainly, in warm climates, the female will call more frequently than in this country.

When the female is in season, the symptoms are unmistakable. She becomes more affectionate, rubs herself against your legs (*photo 1 and colour plate 10*), raises her hind-quarters and calls loudly to the toms for attention. She may do this for four to seven days.

Mating
If the cat is an outdoor one, then you can safely

leave the mating to nature: there will be no shortage of suitors. She may select a single mate or accept several but will usually finish up very pregnant.

If the cat is not allowed out, or if you want pedigree kittens, then you will have to take her to a selected stud tom. Your veterinary surgeon will probably be able to advise you on a suitable one.

Impotence
This is due to lack of virility in the male and is rare in the cat.

Cause
Vitamin A deficiency. Change of environment.

Treatment
The vitamin A deficiency can be put right by mixing two or three drops of good-quality cod-liver oil in the daily diet (*photo 2*).

18
Care of the Pregnant Queen

No special attention or diet is needed in the early stage of pregnancy. However, as the kittens develop in the uterus, the queen's appetite will increase. At this stage protein foods are best, meat especially. Excess carbohydrate will make the queen fat and the birth correspondingly difficult.

Calcium and vitamin tablets may be given, but these are not essential if the queen is fed correctly.

Gestation period
In a normal pregnancy, a queen will carry the kittens in her uterus for approximately sixty-five days, though she may quite naturally go several days over her time. Provided she is healthy and well, there is no need to panic but if she goes off-colour, take her to your veterinary surgeon immediately. In the vast majority of cases, however, the births are straightforward.

False pregnancy
Some cats have false pregnancies, even though they haven't been mated. They exhibit all the typical symptoms, swelling of the abdomen, milk in the teats (*photo 1*), making nests, etc., and then after sixty-five days, gradually return to normal without producing kittens. Veterinary surgeons have several treatments available to help this condition since unused milk in the udders can lead to mastitis complications.

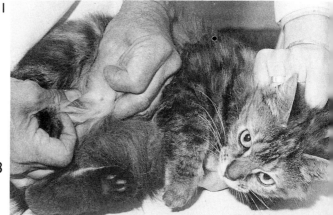

23

19
Preparing for the Birth of the Kittens

In the main, no preparations for the birth are required with the cat, as nature does a near perfect job. Most queens search out a secluded den where they can kit without human interference.

All the owner has to do for an indoor cat is to wait till she selects her spot and then provide an adequate warm bed of newspapers. An outdoor cat will also seek a warm spot within the house.

In addition to seeking out a nest, the queen will present other symptoms. She will become more affectionate and her teats will fill up with milk (*photo 1*).

When labour starts she will disappear into her selected den and **from then on she is best left completely alone for at least 24 hours**. The odd spoiled cat may demand the owner's presence, but fortunately such cases are few.

Often I have to chastise well-meaning owners who phone at 2 or 3 a.m. to say that the cat has

1

been straining for half an hour or an hour with nothing showing. I order the owners straight to bed, and the following morning they have nearly always been presented with a normal litter.

Birth and aftercare
I have found over the years that the entire job is best left to the mother cat (*photo 2*).

The kittens will usually be born head first and enclosed in a sac followed by an afterbirth. The mother will open the sac, clean the kitten with her rough tongue, bite through the navel cord if necessary and eat the afterbirth. Human interference in this process merely leads to delays and complications.

If, however, the queen has made no progress after 24 hours in the nest, or if a kitten appears stuck, then consult a veterinary surgeon immediately. Posterior presentations, with the tail coming first, sometimes require a little help.

2

Caesarean section
Caesarean section in the cat is rarely necessary. In fact a friend of mine, a former Professor of surgery in a Scottish Veterinary University, told me after he had spent thirty years in small animal practice that in his opinion it is never necessary. Certainly the cat has an amazing capacity for prolonged labour and will often pass a dead kitten several days after the main litter has been born.

However, I think that a caesarean section is

probably justified in prolonged labour in a pedigree queen where live kittens are a vital economic necessity (*photo 3*). The operation is not excessively difficult and is highly successful.

Sexing the kittens

This is not so difficult as is generally thought, though it requires considerable experience. It is done by an assessment of the relative distances between the anal and urethral orifices (openings). In the female the two openings are comparatively close to each other. In the male they are wider apart.

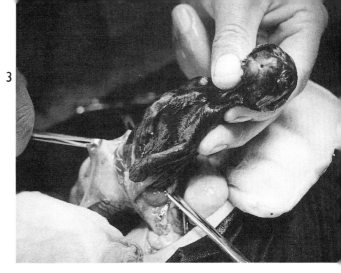

3

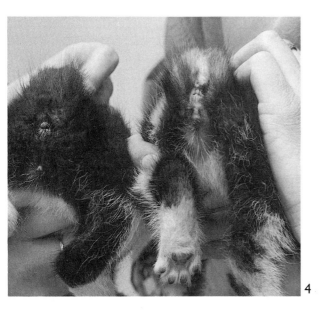

4

Some people say it is easier to sex kittens before the fur starts to grow; personally I think it is only easy when you have a female in one hand and a male in the other (*photo 4*).

Weaning

A kitten's teeth appear during the second week, and by the third it shows an interest in solid food.

Under natural conditions the kittens are weaned from the queen at six weeks, and from three weeks onwards they progressively share the same food as the mother.

If, for any reason, early weaning is necessary, the kittens should be given special milk (*photo 5*) at three weeks with perhaps some added cereal and finely minced raw beef or hard-boiled egg from four weeks onwards. Small quantities given frequently are the ideal. Feed to appetite, giving

only as much as they will clear up five or six times a day.

At eight weeks they will still need three feeds daily and subsequently at least two feeds every twenty-four hours until they are adult at nine or ten months, when they can go on to once-daily feeding, though personally I prefer to continue with two feeds throughout the cat's life.

Eclampsia — Milk Fever

This is rare in the queen.

Cause

Calcium deficiency, due to suckling an excessively large litter.

Symptoms

The symptoms appear when the kittens are between three and eight weeks old. The queen starts to stagger, shiver and breathe heavily. If untreated, she loses the power of her legs and goes into a coma. The temperature may rise to 109°F (43°C).

Treatment

See your veterinary surgeon, who will remove the kittens immediately and inject the queen with calcium, intravenously and subcutaneously.

5

20
Rearing Orphan Kittens

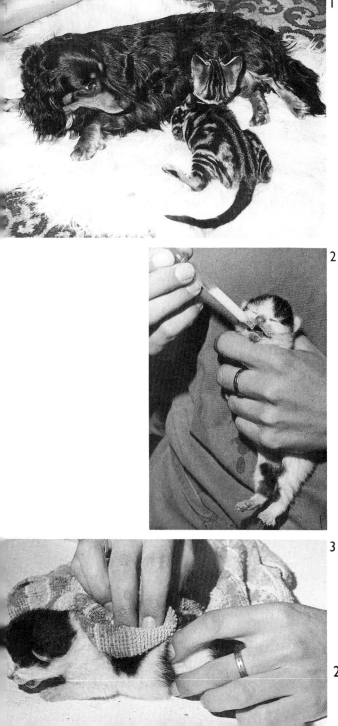

1

2

3

The best way to rear orphan kittens is on a foster mother, and the 'mother' needn't be a cat. I've known several lactating bitches that have taken to kittens without any trouble (*photo 1*). Faced with the problem, always consult your veterinary surgeon: he is the most likely to know where a foster parent can be found.

Hand-rearing of orphans requires not only patience and determination but a considerable amount of good luck together with infinite care.

In the early hours of life the kittens require warmth above everything else — a temperature of 90°F (32°C) for the first twenty-four hours, and 80°–85°F (27°–29°C) for the next fortnight. To obtain this, an infra-red lamp may be needed.

After a fortnight the temperature can be dropped to 70°F (21°C) — i.e., warm room temperature.

Cow's milk is too strong for kittens. Baby milk at twice the recommended strength is much better. If none is available, then the kittens can be started on a special formula comprising:
    3 parts cow's milk
    1 part lime water
    2 drops cod-liver oil
    2 teaspoonfuls of glucose
Add half-a-teaspoonful of beef extract and feed at body temperature, i.e., 101.5°F (38.5°C).

The kittens will have to be fed every three hours with a doll's feeding bottle or an eye dropper (*photo 2*). Don't force the milk down; merely allow the kittens to suck their fill.

After each feed rub the kittens' bellies with a coarse, damp warm towel (*photo 3*). This will stimulate their digestive system and help them to urinate and pass motions. Provide a clean bed of newspapers three times a day.

From three weeks onwards follow the instructions already given for weaning.

As soon as the orphans start to stagger away from their nest, introduce them to a litter tray.

At all times, don't hesitate to ring your veterinary surgeon for advice and help.

A hand-reared kitten as a pet
I have often heard it said that a hand-reared kitten does not make a good pet. This has not been my experience. It may be more prone to infections during the first year of life because of lack of antibodies that would normally have been obtained from the mother's colostrum (first milk), but thereafter I have found such animals normal.

Reports of viciousness and behavioural problems are probably coincidental.

Kittens rejected by the mother
Some veterinary surgeons advise euthanasia of the rejected kitten. Personally I advise giving the unfortunate creature every possible chance of survival.

Health, Disease and General Conditions

21
The Eyes

Conjunctivitis
Conjunctivitis simply means inflammation of the conjunctiva, the delicate membrane which covers and protects the eye (*photo 1*).

Cause
In the cat the main cause is pollen or dust getting into the eyes during the cat's travels through long grass or undergrowth. The pollen or dust produces an irritation which allows bacteria to start to multiply.

Sometimes the trigger cause is a foreign body, grass seed or oat husk on the eye surface (*photo 2*) or lodged underneath the nictitating membrane (third eyelid).

The respiratory virus of cat flu and an organism called *Chlamydia* also attack the conjunctiva and may cause a chronic conjunctivitis.

Symptoms
Profuse lacrymation. Tears run down the cheek from the affected eye, and within a day or two if untreated, the eye will partially or completely

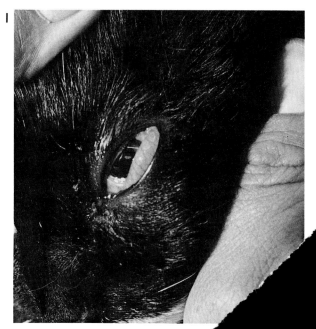

close and mucus or yellow pus will
corner of the eye and along the

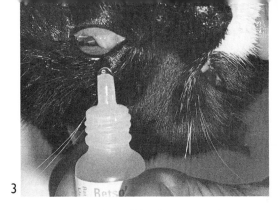

2

(*photo 4 and colour plate 11*); then wipe the discharge from the lids and corners with the same swab.

3

Treatment

A prompt visit to your veterinary surgeon. He will examine the eye carefully, probably under local anaesthesia. If a foreign body is present, he will remove it and prescribe an appropriate antibiotic ointment or drops for daily or twice daily application (*photo 3*).

As a first-aid measure the eye can be bathed with warm normal saline solution (two teaspoonfuls of common salt to one litre of warm water). Hold a piece of cotton wool soaked in the solution above the cat's eye and squeeze

4

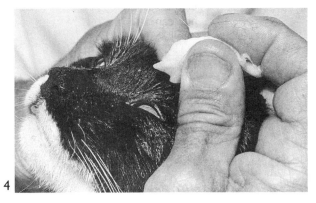

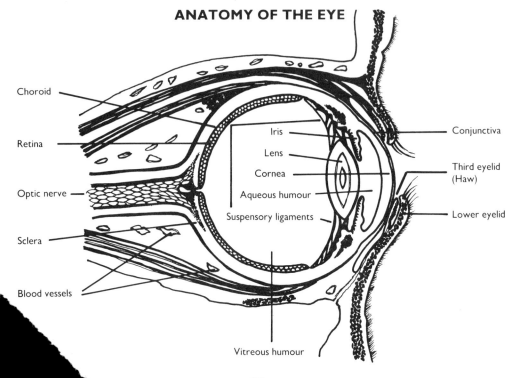

ANATOMY OF THE EYE

Choroid

Retina

Optic nerve

Sclera

Blood vessels

Iris

Lens

Cornea

Aqueous humour

Suspensory ligaments

Conjunctiva

Third eyelid (Haw)

Lower eyelid

Vitreous humour

Old-fashioned remedies like cold tea are unsatisfactory, and in any case a precise diagnosis by your veterinary surgeon is vital before successful treatment can be started.

Keratitis

Keratitis means inflammation of the cornea, i.e., the tough membrane which covers the central surface of the eye (*see diagram*).

Cause

It may flare up secondary to a bacterial conjunctivitis or it may be caused by direct injury by accident or a foreign body.

Vitamin A deficiency can also cause keratitis.

When the surface cells of the cornea are damaged, an ulcer develops which may become infected.

Symptoms

The cornea clouds over (*photo 5*). The cat blinks repeatedly or keeps the eye tightly closed. There is a watery discharge quickly developing into mucus or pus. The blood vessels of the sclera (the white of the eye) become congested. There is considerable pain, especially when bacteria are involved.

Treatment

As for conjunctivitis, though with keratitis prompt veterinary attention is even more vital (*colour plate 12*).

Squint (Strabismus)

This occurs when the cat's eyeballs move independently of each other. Squinting need not necessarily impede the vision; in fact it seldom does except when secondary to injury or tumour formation.

Cause

Usually a hereditary weakness, especially in the Siamese breed. Other less frequent causes are direct injury to the muscles or nerves controlling the eyeball, and tumour formation in the eye socket.

Treatment

Very much a job for a veterinary surgeon. In hereditary cases he will probably advise leaving well alone. With tumours or irreparable damage he will remove the eye.

5

6

Glaucoma

Glaucoma is a distension of the eyeball due to an excessive accumulation of fluid within the eye (*photo 6*). One or both eyes may be affected.

Cause

The cornea of the eye is nourished by a fluid called lymph. Glaucoma may be caused by an excessive supply of lymph, but more usually it is brought about by an interference with the lymph drainage.

Such interference may have a congenital or primary origin, but more often it is secondary to eye damage or disease. Most of the cat cases I've seen have been associated with dislocation of the

7

lens into the anterior chamber. Such a dislocation certainly prevents adequate drainage.

When the distension reaches a certain stage, the cat may have considerable pain in addition to being blind in the affected eye.

Treatment
Very much a job for the veterinary surgeon. In the early stages, he will probably prescribe drops called Timoptol.

If, as is usually the case, the condition has been present for some time, the distension can be relieved by a delicate operation comprising puncturing the cornea at the sclera-conjunctival border, withdrawing a portion of the iris and suturing it to the conjunctiva. This produces a permanent fistula or surface drainage hole.

I've also had considerable success by removing the dislocated lens.

The drug called Timoptol and 1% Pilocarpine eye drops help to relieve the condition and the drops have to be continued after the operation is performed.

In advanced cases, especially if the cornea ruptures, the eye has to be removed.

Entropion
Entropion occurs when the eyelids become inverted. The condition is nothing like as common in cats as it is in dogs. The odd cases I have seen have been associated with congenitally small eyes, though entropion can be due to a scratch or bite wound.

Symptoms
The inverted lid rubs over the surface of the eye producing a traumatic conjunctivitis, keratitis or ulceration with all the typical signs already described (*photo 7*).

Treatment
Your veterinary surgeon can operate quickly and successfully provided the eye damage is not excessive. So, once again, get suspect cases to the veterinary surgeon as soon as possible.

Ectropion
This means eversion of the eyelids. This is even more uncommon in the cat than entropion. No congenital cases have been recorded and the odd case will be secondary to a wound.

Treatment
The veterinary surgeon can correct the deformity by simple plastic surgery.

Blocked Tear Duct
Fortunately this is rarely seen in cats.

Cause
Usually secondary to a severe or chronic eye infection (conjunctivitis or keratitis).

Symptoms
A persistently watering eye with a well-marked dark stain down one side of the cheek (*photo 8*).

8

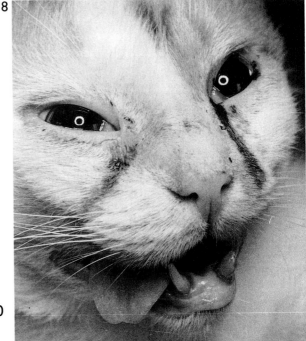

Treatment

Your veterinary surgeon will anaesthetise the cat and attempt to clear the duct using fine nylon or fluid pressure (*photo 9*).

Cataract

This is an opacity or clouding over of the crystalline lens of the eye (*photo 10*). It is uncommon in the cat, though it can occur congenitally.

Cause

Chiefly old age though any condition that interferes with the nutrition of the lens can cause it such as direct injury to the eye or pressure from glaucoma or tumours. It can also occur in diabetes (see Diabetes, page 74).

Treatment

Very much a condition for your veterinary surgeon.

Surgical removal of the affected lens in certain cases can be successful with apparent restoration of partial vision, and replacement with a plastic lens, as in humans, has been recently achieved.

Haw

This is the name given to the condition where the third eyelid or membrana nictitans (nictitating membrane) comes partially over the eye (*photo 11 and colour plate 13*).

Cause

Haw is usually an indication that the cat is out of sorts and requires veterinary attention. I've seen the condition often associated with mild gastro-intestinal upsets.

9

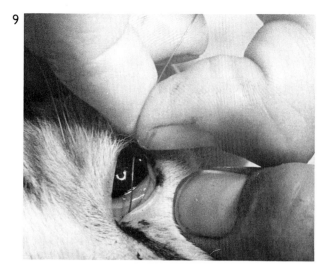

10

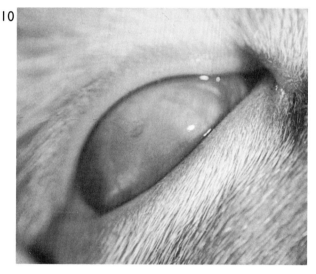

Treatment

The membrana nictitans almost invariably goes back as soon as the cat regains normal health, though occasionally I've seen it persist in overweight lazy cats for no apparent reason.

It should be regarded only as a symptom rather than a disease.

One home treatment which I've found beneficial is a pinch of baking soda (sodium bicarbonate) in the drinking water or milk.

11

Removal of the eye

This drastic operation may be necessary if the eye is excessively damaged, badly infected or grossly distended (as in some advanced cases of glaucoma) with rupture of the cornea.

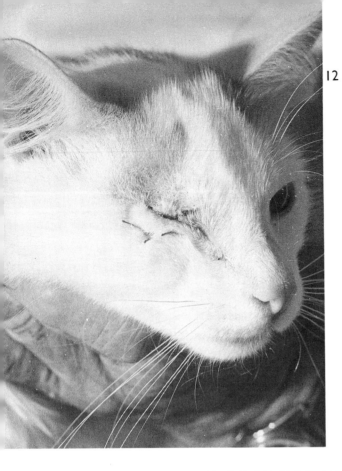

The decision and operation (*photo 12*) must always of course be left to your veterinary surgeon.

General information

Kittens

I am often asked how long it takes kittens' eyes to open after birth. The answer is normally six to twelve days, though certain breeds like the Siamese may open as early as the second or third day.

Colour sight

As stated earlier, cats are not colour blind though their colour sense is not so well developed as that of humans. Research has shown that they can distinguish green and blue but not red.

Eye ulcers

Ulcers on the eye surface are due to either direct injury or a chronic untreated infection. To avoid the latter seek veterinary attention at the slightest sign of eye trouble.

22
The Ears

Otitis

Otitis (so-called 'canker') simply means inflammation of the lining membrane of the ear, and the part most commonly affected is the external portion or what we call the *otitis externa* (*photo 1 and colour plate 14*).

Causes

In order of frequency in my experience:
  Infestation by ear mites (mange mites) (*see diagram*)
  Infection by bacteria
  Foreign bodies — grass seeds, small stones, etc.

Symptoms

Shaking the head and persistent scratching.

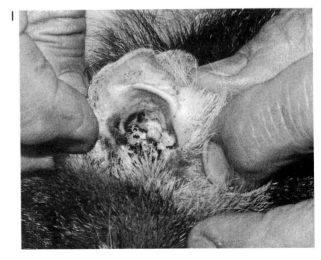

THE EAR MITE

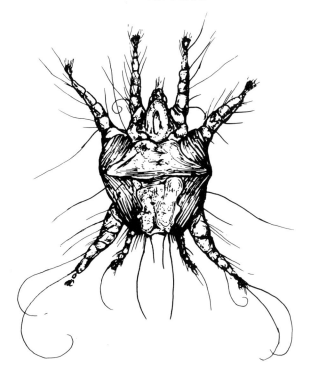

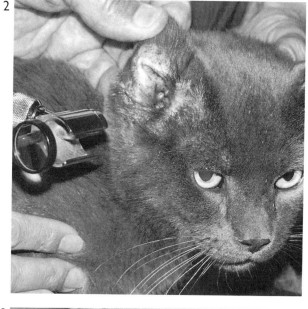

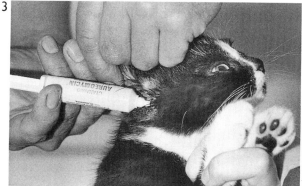

Treatment

Your veterinary surgeon will diagnose the cause by using an auroscope (*photo 2*) and will apply and prescribe the correct therapy. If mange mites are present, he will clean the ears carefully and prescribe gammexane drops every second day for at least a fortnight (*colour plate 15*), since the mites burrow into the ear lining and lay eggs which take ten to fourteen days to hatch out.

If the otitis is due to infection, he may syringe the ear with warm antiseptic solution and follow up with daily insertions of a suitable antibiotic dressing (*photo 3*).

If a foreign body is present, he may have to anaesthetise the cat to remove it.

Middle and inner ear infections

Cats have a well-developed middle and inner ear which occasionally becomes infected.

Cause

Extension of infection from the external ear.

Symptoms

The patient suffers considerable pain and is usually

off food. There is a staggering gait, and the head may be rotated or held to one side; occasionally the cat falls over repeatedly when walking, or consistently turns in one direction (*photo 4*).

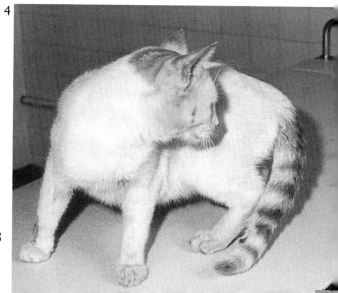

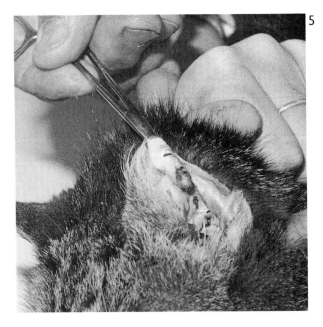

5

It is not an easy condition to cure, and the cat may be left with a permanent uncertain gait, but prompt surgery relieves the pain and this is of paramount importance.

Cleaning ears

One very important point — the lining of the ear is delicate and sensitive — and on no account should an owner attempt to clean it out with cotton wool or other probes. Any such interference will only worsen the ear condition.

The cleaning of ears should always be left to the skilled hands of the veterinary surgeon (*photo 5 and colour plate 16*).

Haematoma

An aural (ear) haematoma is a pronounced swelling of the external ear flap (*photo 6*). The swelling, as the name indicates, contains blood.

Cause

Persistent scratching or head shaking, due to untreated otitis, causes numerous small blood vessels between the flap and the skin to rupture.

Treatment

If the haematoma is small, treatment of the otitis may be all that is required but usually the veterinary surgeon has to operate, using a general anaesthesia. He removes a rectangular or elliptical portion from the inner wall of the ear flap (*photo 7*), releases the blood and blood clots, then sutures through the flap.

6

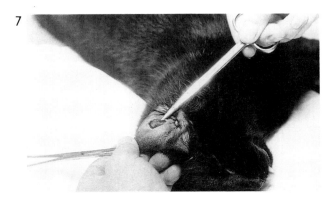

7

Treatment

This should be left entirely to your veterinary surgeon.

He will anaesthetise the cat, open through the ear drum to permit drainage and prescribe broad-spectrum antibiotics and steroids.

The operation is successful only if the original cause of the irritation is treated and cured.

Deafness

Deafness in a young cat is usually associated with white fur colour (albino) and is thought to be hereditary (*photo 8*).

Deafness in old age is caused by senile ossification within the middle ear.

Temporary and partial deafness may be secondary to or associated with ear infections.

Treatment and prevention

Avoid the purchase of an albino and never neglect an ear condition. A single visit to your veterinary surgeon may be all that is necessary.

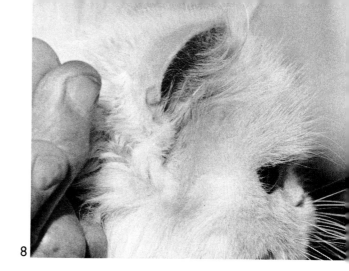

8

23
The Nasal Chambers

The external nostrils are linked to the pharynx (throat) by the nasal cavities.

The nasal chambers or sinuses act as a bacterial and dust filter to protect the lungs from infection. They contain delicate bones covered by a moist layer of mucous membrane. Small hairs, called cilia, protrude from the membrane and beat continuously to keep the mucus moving across the surface; this mucus traps the dust and bacteria and warms the air before it passes into the lungs.

Catarrh or 'snuffles'

A common condition.

Cause

Trigger factor is one of the flu viruses which damages the nasal mucosa and allows secondary bacteria, like streptococci, chlamydiae and staphylococci, to grow. It is the bacteria which produce the pus that is associated with nasal catarrh.

Symptoms

Persistent frequent attacks of sneezing accompanied by either a watery (*photo 1*) or a profuse thick catarrhal discharge. The appetite becomes capricious; usually there is no fever.

1

Treatment

Early cases respond quickly to long-acting or broad-spectrum antibiotics.

Sinusitis

Sinusitis develops fairly rapidly if the early

35

symptoms are neglected. A mucopurulent discharge persists from one nostril (*photo 2*).

Cause

Extension of the infection into the upper nasal chambers.

Treatment

If the condition does not clear up with prolonged antibiotic therapy, then an operation is necessary.

Under a general anaesthetic the veterinary surgeon will drill (trephine) into the top nasal chamber called the frontal sinus (*photo 3*) and will irrigate the sinuses for several successive days with antibiotic solutions. More than one operation may be necessary to effect a complete cure.

2

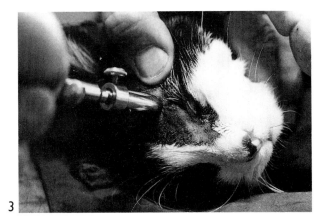

3

24
The Mouth

Bad breath

This is not uncommon but is encountered mainly in older cats.

Cause

Neglected teeth, plaque, tartar, decay, pyorrhoea, mouth infection and ulcers are the main causes, though digestive upsets can be responsible.

Vitamin B deficiency can also give rise to bad breath, as can nephritis (see page 62).

Treatment

A visit to your veterinary surgeon, who will diagnose the trouble and remove the cause (*colour plate 17*). He may well prescribe an oral antibiotic and a course of vitamin B.

Wounds

Because of the one-way papillae on the cat's tongue, mouth wounds do occur, especially in kittens (*photo 1*).

I

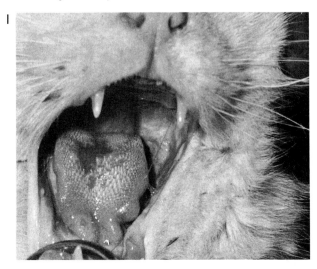

Symptoms

Loss of appetite and dribbling at the mouth.

Treatment

Get your veterinary surgeon to make sure there is no sharp foreign body, like a needle, stuck in the mouth or pharynx. Even if there isn't, a single injection of long-acting antibiotic will help rapid healing without infection.

Gingivitis

This means simply inflammation of the gums (*colour plate 18*).

Cause

In my experience, the main predisposing cause is the accumulation of tartar on the teeth; the tartar presses on the gums, producing a distinct reddening around the base of the teeth crowns. Another cause is the licking of irritants like creosote. It is also sometimes seen in five- to six-month-old kittens when the permanent teeth are coming through.

Symptoms

Capricious appetite, difficulty in eating and occasionally slobbering. A distinct red line of inflammation may develop between the teeth and gums (*photo 2*).

Treatment

Gingivitis is not easy to clear up and requires a veterinary surgeon to diagnose and remove the cause before prescribing the correct treatment.

Pyorrhoea (peridontal disease)

This occurs when an infection develops at the junction of the crown and root of the teeth (*photo 3*). The infection extends into the alveoli or teeth cavities.

Cause

Plaque, tartar or tooth decay which allows bacteria to enter and multiply (*colour plate 19*).

Symptoms

A vile smell from the mouth, though the appetite may not be impaired. Examination shows lines of greyish pus between the gums and the teeth.

Treatment

If reasonable care and attention has been paid to

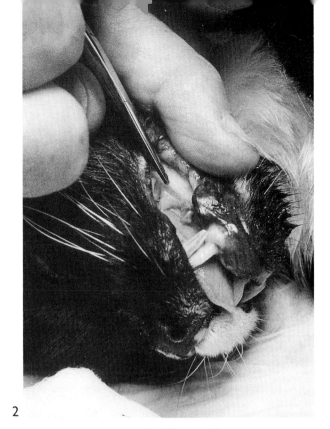

2

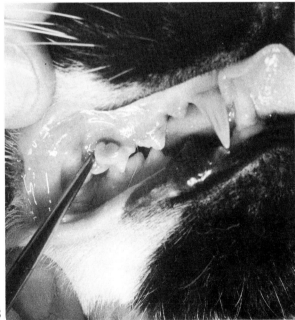

3

your pet, pyorrhoea should not be allowed to develop. However, if you suspect it, take your cat to your veterinary surgeon at once.

He will clean up the mouth and perhaps remove a few teeth. Then he'll probably prescribe a course of oral antibiotics.

Benign ulcer

A benign ulcer simply means an ulcer which is not malignant (*photo 4*).

Cause

The main cause in the cat is excessive tartar formation on the teeth, which lacerates the mucous membrane of the adjacent part of the lip or jaw. It can also be caused by an irritant poison.

Benign ulcers form on the mouth and tongue secondary to acute virus infections or to chronic kidney disease.

5

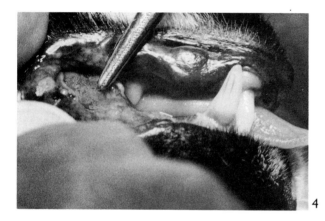

4

Symptoms

An unpleasant odour with or without slobbering from the mouth. The ulcer can be clearly seen when the mouth is examined carefully. Again, this is a job for your veterinary surgeon as is the treatment of the condition.

Prevention

In the main the majority of benign ulcers can be avoided by having the cat's teeth examined and scaled yearly from middle age onwards (that is, from four years).

Rodent ulcer

For many years this was thought to be cancerous (malignant).

It appears on the skin of the lip region and can affect adult cats at any age (*photo 5*).

Cause

The rodent ulcer of cats is now thought to be due to a chronic low-grade bacterial infection of the skin aggravated by contact with the rough surface of the tongue.

Symptoms

A small, shiny and slightly depressed ulcer appears near the centre of the upper lip — sometimes immediately below the nostrils. The ulcer gradually erodes the surrounding tissue, producing salivation and difficulty in eating.

Treatment

I've had considerable success with large doses of long-acting steroids combined with long-acting antibiotics and the use of cryo-surgery (*photo 6*). A course of six injections at five-day intervals has cleared several rodent ulcers completely.

The ideal therapy is irradiation, but unfortunately facilities for this are scarce.

Before the days of antibiotics and steroids I used to remove the ulcers surgically immediately I saw them. I had some success but mostly they flared up again by extending into the surrounding tissues.

Ranula

Sometimes called a honey cyst, ranula is the name given to an enlarged sublingual salivary gland. It is not common in the cat.

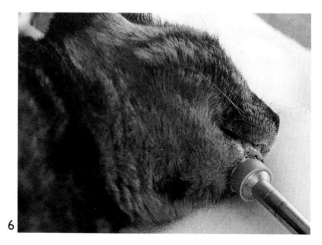

6

Cause
Usually secondary to an infection of the mouth producing a blockage of the salivary ducts.

Treatment
Consult your veterinary surgeon. A general anaesthetic will be required and the veterinary surgeon will probably remove the offending salivary gland. Some prefer to drain the swelling and cauterise the inside with strong iodine solution or silver nitrate. Personally I prefer complete removal.

25
The Teeth

A cat gets a full mouth of thirty permanent teeth around seven months of age; twelve incisors at four months; four canines at four-and-a-half months; and fourteen molars between six and seven months. Thereafter, for the next couple of years the cat's teeth remain well-nigh perfect.

Tartar
Dental plaque or deposit (*photo 1*) and tartar (*photo 2*) may start to form from three years onwards.

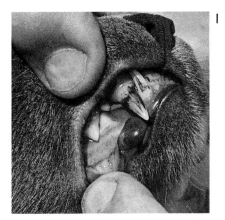

I

2

CROSS-SECTION OF THE CAT'S TOOTH

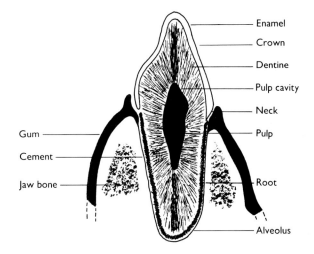

Enamel
Crown
Dentine
Pulp cavity
Neck
Gum
Cement
Jaw bone
Pulp
Root
Alveolus

Cause
Not fully understood, but it is thought to be associated with the degree of alkalinity or acidity in the saliva. There certainly must be some predisposing factor in individual cats, since the majority maintain clean, healthy teeth into old age.

Treatment
Have your cat's teeth inspected by a veterinary surgeon every year from the age of four onwards. If necessary, he will clean and scale the teeth (*photo 3*). Delayed tartar removal leads to gingivitis, pyorrhoea and tooth decay.

39

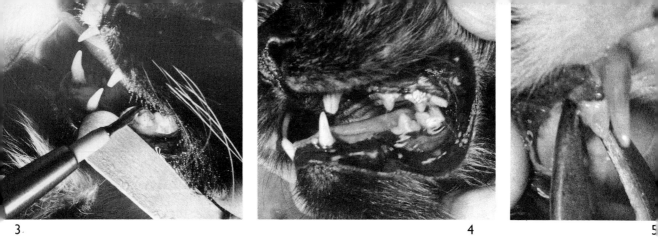

Caries

This means disintegration of the enamel (*photo 4*). Caries is not common in the cat; in the last twenty years I've seen only two cases.

Cause

Probably a congenital predisposition exacerbated by a calcium deficiency.

Symptoms

Reluctance to eat and salivation.

Treatment

Calcium tablets and soft foods.

Decay

Tooth decay is nearly always due to neglect.

Symptoms

Stinking breath and capricious appetite.

Treatment

Removal (*photo 5*) and scaling under general anaesthetic.

Prevention

Regular inspection by your veterinary surgeon.

26
External Parasites

The common external parasites found in cats are:

Fleas	Mites
Lice	Ticks
Fungi	Maggots

Fleas

Three species are found on cats:

Ctenocephalides felis — the cat flea
Ctenocephalides canis — the dog flea
Pulex irritans — the human flea

Symptoms

Fleas seem to affect some cats worse than others, probably because their skins vary in sensitivity.

Also there seems little doubt that some cats are allergic to flea saliva.

In general, the outstanding symptoms are scratching (*photo 1*), biting and twitching of the skin. Examination of the coat may show the odd flea darting for cover, but the degree of infestation can often be judged by the presence along the back of hard black or brown granules (*photo 2*). These are not flea eggs, as so many people think, but are hardened pellets of the flea's faeces; the dark brown or black colour comes from the haemoglobin of the flea's blood-sucking activities. Raw moist areas of allergic eczema may appear.

So long as the fleas have a ready host to feed on

1

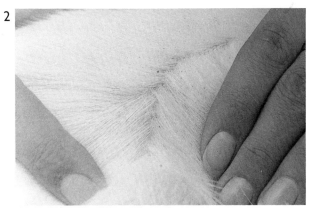

2

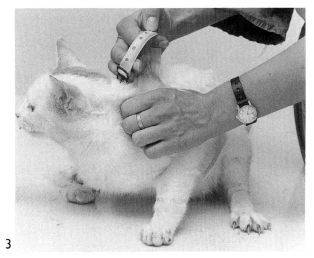

3

they can live for up to two years and they can cause a lot of itching in that time. Adult fleas can also act as intermediate hosts of tapeworms (see Internal Parasites, page 48).

Treatment
The important thing to remember is that, except with the occasional long-haired cat, part of a flea's life cycle takes place off the cat, namely on the cat's bedding and on household carpets and furniture. Therefore, in order to clear up an infestation completely one has to treat the bedding, carpets and furniture as well as the cat.

Powerful aerosol sprays are now available for both the patient and its habitat, but a reputable parasitic dusting powder is equally efficient. The veterinary surgeon will supply the necessary.

If the cat, like the vast majority of them, has access to the outside world, it is wise to bear in mind that reinfestation can happen at any time. Cat flea collars (*photo 3*) may help considerably but they afford only a partial protection. As such effective modern treatments are now available, I advise against flea collars in adult agile cats because of the danger of strangulation during outdoor hunting.

Lice
Fortunately lice infestation is not common in healthy cats. Personally I've seen it only in poorly fed kittens and disease-debilitated adults.

Cause
Two types of louse may attack a cat:

The biting lice — *Trichodectes canis* (*see diagram on page 42*) and *Felicola subrostrato*

The sucking louse — *Ligognathus setosus*

Common sites for the parasites are the head and inside the forelegs. The entire louse life cycle takes place on the cat.

Symptoms
Unthriftiness and itching, though scratching and biting are not so marked as with fleas.

The lice can be easily seen in scurfy areas. They are bluish-grey and oval and about the size of a pin-head.

Lice eggs (nits) are laid on the cat and attach themselves to the hair.

Treatment
As for fleas, thorough dusting or spraying should

be continued weekly until all the nits have disappeared. Only the cat requires treatment, though the bedding should be burned daily.

A BITING LOUSE

Fungi

Two species of ringworm fungi can invade the skin, hair or claws of a cat. These cause the condition of ringworm, and they are called *Microsporon canis* and *Trichophyton mentagrophytes*. Healthy adult cats can carry the fungi without showing symptoms.

The ringworm fungi are zoonotic and thus can affect humans.

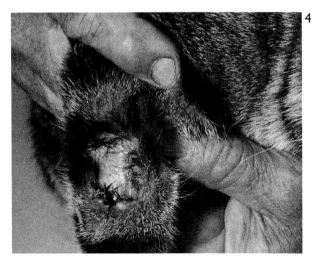

4

Symptoms

Cat ringworm (like lice infestation) is seen mainly in poorly fed young kittens or malnourished or debilitated adults. It tends to break out around the forehead, ears, feet or legs.

Acute moist or irritating dry circular patches appear in the coat and if untreated spread out peripherally (*photo 4*).

Treatment

Take the cat straight to your veterinary surgeon. He will confirm the diagnosis by using a special lamp (*photo 5*) and will prescribe Griseofulvin tablets with or without oral antibiotics. Treated promptly, the condition will clear up in a fortnight.

5
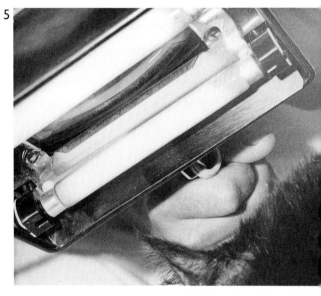

All bedding should be destroyed daily; sleeping areas require flaming over with a blowlamp at least twice during the oral treatment.

Local dressings on the cat are not very effective and can be dangerous especially if they contain iodine or mercury.

NB. A pregnant queen may have to wait till the kittens are born before Griseofulvin treatment.

Mites

Five different mites can attack the cat:
    Otodectic cynotis
    Notoedres cati
    The harvest mite — *Trombiculid autumnalis*
    Two mites of the *Cheyletiella* group

Otodectic cynotis
This causes ear mange, which has already been dealt with (see The Ears).

Just one other important point. These ear mites can be passed from cat to cat and cat to dog and vice versa. So, if you have a dog in the house and more than one cat, then it is wise to treat them all simultaneously.

Notoedres cati
This causes head mange.

Symptoms
The mite burrows into the skin of the head or neck, though if untreated, it can spread to the whole body. Most of the cases I've seen have started at the base of one ear (*photo 6*).

The irritation produced by the burrowing of the mites causes intense scratching and rubbing of the area. The patient may literally 'rub itself raw'. The hair drops out and pustules may develop due to secondary infection by bacteria.

Treatment
A veterinary surgeon will be required to diagnose and treat the condition. Twice weekly applications of special mange lotions will clear the condition up in a month provided it is localised when treatment commences.

The harvest mite (see diagram)
This can attack cats during the months of July, August and September, but apparently only in certain parts of the country.

Symptoms
Between the cat's toes (*photo 7*) and on the surface of the belly the mites insert small hooked fangs into the skin to feed. This causes an irritation which the cat makes worse by persistent licking.

Raw moist areas covered by a hard scab form.

Occasionally, the mite attaches itself to the short-haired areas of the head or groin.

Treatment
Derris or gammexane dusting powder combined with oral steroids will clear the condition up rapidly, but only your veterinary surgeon will be able to diagnose the condition correctly.

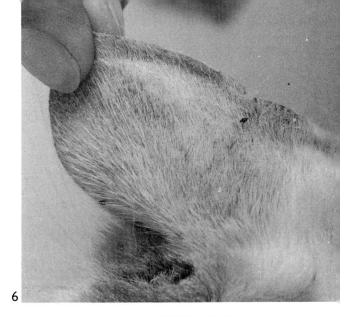
6

THE HARVEST MITE

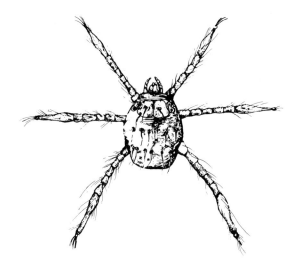

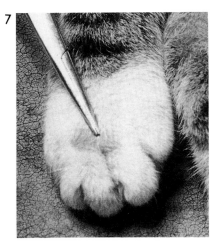
7

8

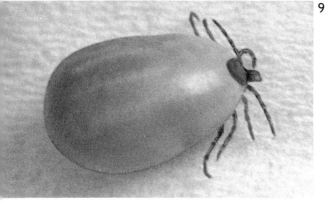

9

The Cheyletiella *group*
These do not burrow into the cat's skin but lay their eggs at the root of the hairs. The cat picks these mites up from rabbits or from where rabbits have been lying.

Symptoms
Large amounts of scurf or dandruff. The mites, which can be seen with the naked eye, move about among the dandruff scales. So if you comb the dandruff out onto some white paper and see the mites (*photo 8*), then consult your veterinary surgeon at once.

Treatment
Highly satisfactory, comprising the use of a special parasitical shampoo.

Ticks
The common species of tick found in this country is the *Ixodes ricinus* (*photo 9*). It occurs mostly in

certain geographical areas such as Scotland and the hills of northern England.
All warm-blooded animals including cats can become infested, and odd cases can appear anywhere.

Symptoms
The ticks attach themselves mainly to the head and legs of the cat and slowly engorge themselves with the host's blood. They apparently cause little irritation, since owners often mistake them for small tumours or cysts, and only when the owners actually see the ticks are veterinary surgeons usually called to treat them.

Treatment
The ticks can only be satisfactorily removed after they have been anaesthetised by ether or chloroform. If pulled off forcibly, the head will be left buried in the skin and may lead to an infected sore.

Prevention
In tick areas the cat can be protected by fortnightly dusting with a parasitic powder supplied by your veterinary surgeon.
It is probably wise to dust over the cat's sleeping quarters at the same time.

Maggots (myiasis)
Cause
The predisposing cause is dirt such as dried faeces and urine around the anus and urethra (*photo 10*). In cats such dirt is more likely to form in the long-

10

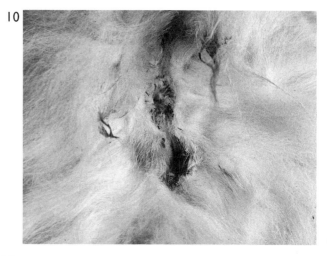

haired breeds, especially in an old or infirm cat which has become casual with its toilet. The green bottle fly lays its eggs on the filth and the eggs develop into larvae or maggots (*photo 11*).

Symptoms
An affected cat quickly loses appetite and interest and develops a most unpleasant odour. These symptoms are due to toxins excreted by the maggots, excess of which can kill the cat.

Treatment
Immediate veterinary attention is vital, since the maggots can and do burrow into and live on living tissues. All visible larvae have to be removed — the area thoroughly cleansed with a non-irritant antiseptic solution or with cotton wool soaked in chloroform. A powerful anti-fly agent such as gammexane sheep dip then has to be applied.

Unless treatment is quickly carried out, the cat may have to be put to sleep.

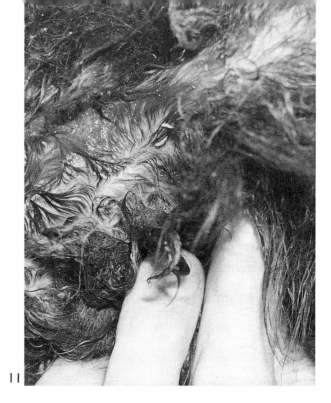

11

27
Skin Diseases

Alopecia
Alopecia simply means a loss of hair or baldness.

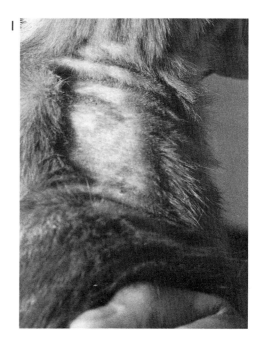

1

Cause
Hormonal inbalance or upset of relative hormone levels in the bloodstream. Such upset occurs mainly in neutered cats. Occasionally it is hereditary.

Symptoms
The loss of hair usually starts around the rear end or head of the cat (*photo 1*) and inside the thighs. From there, if untreated, it extends along the belly.

In the congenital form, called *Alopecia congenita*, the bald patches are spread over the entire body, while the rest of the coat is sparse. As the cat gets older the skin becomes completely bare and wrinkled.

Treatment
The hormonal type responds well to daily doses of

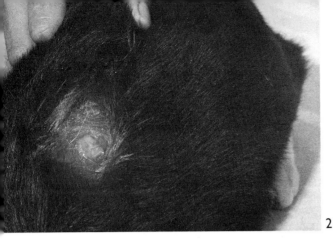

the correct hormones. Your veterinary surgeon will advise and prescribe.

There is no treatment for the congenital cases.

Eczema

Eczema is the name loosely applied to most skin conditions and the differential diagnosis of the various types is not always easy (*photo 2*).

2

Flea eczema

3

Cause

A heavy infestation of fleas.

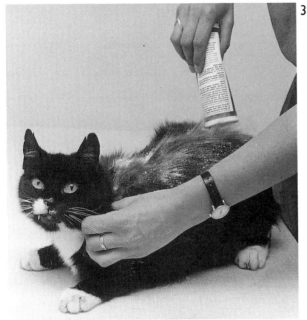

Symptoms

Patches of the skin become covered by a brownish deposit and these patches become moist and raw as the cat bites and licks at them. The sight of the fleas or the presence of the dark granules of flea faeces in the coat completes the usual picture.

Treatment

Get rid of the fleas and the skin condition will soon clear up.

Dust or spray the coat thoroughly with a safe parasitical agent obtained from your veterinary surgeon. Repeat twice at 14-day intervals (*photo 3*).

At the same time, use newspapers for the cat's bedding and burn them every day. Also dust or spray over and vacuum the various spots in the house where the cat normally lies (*photo 4*). This is an important precaution, since the life-cycle of the flea takes place not on the cat (except on the occasional long-haired breeds) but on the surrounding furniture where the flea eggs feed on micro-organisms present in dust or dirt until they develop into adult fleas.

4

Other parasitic eczemas

These are much milder than flea eczema and have already been described under external parasites, namely, lice infestation and infestation by the *Cheyletiella* mite which is characterised by excess scurf or dandruff.

Allergic eczemas

Cause

In most cases the cause is complex. The condition may or may not be dietetical. Sometimes it appears in cats fed entirely on fish, hence the term 'Fish eczema', though personally I doubt whether fish feeding is a direct trigger factor. Often a hormonal inbalance or a vitamin B deficiency is involved.

Symptoms
Small scabby spots develop along the back and sides (*photo 5*). The patient licks the spots persistently, producing raw moist lesions which gradually extend. If the condition is not treated successfully, the scabs appear over the entire body.

5

Treatment
Diagnosis and treatment of this complex condition should be left entirely to your veterinary surgeon.

Personally I've had most success with female hormone implants combined with vitamin B injections and thyroid extract tablets given by the mouth. The initial severe itching is relieved considerably by injecting long-acting cortisone.

At the same time a change of diet is recommended.

Mange
There are two types:
Otodectic mange (*photo 6*)
Notoedric mange
Both of these have already been dealt with under External Parasites.

Ringworm
See section on fungi, page 42.

Cancer of the skin
This is rare in the cat and has to be diagnosed by a skin specialist. Any chronic skin condition will probably be referred by your own vet to a specialist at one of the universities.

Sweating
Although the skin of a cat contains glands histologically identical to our own sweat glands, the cat perspires only from the pads of the feet and then mainly when frightened.

As in the dog, the main heat loss is effected by panting.

Warts
Warts are benign growths of the skin (sometimes called papillomas).

6

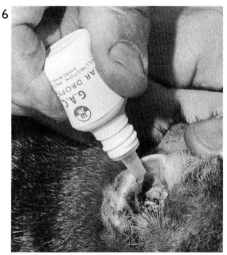

Cause
A virus.

Symptoms
The warts may be single or in clusters, mainly around the head, eyes, mouth (*photo 7*), ears, neck, shoulders; just occasionally on the abdomen.

Treatment
Your veterinary surgeon will remove them under a general anaesthetic if or when they become a nuisance.

7

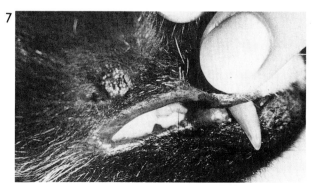

28
Internal Parasites

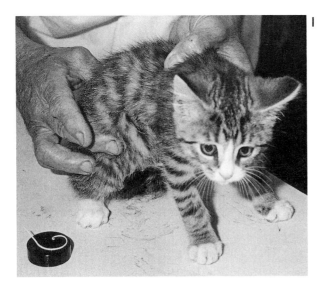

The internal parasites of the cat comprise:
  (1) Roundworms
  (2) Tapeworms

ROUNDWORMS

There are three types:
  Ascarids
  Hookworms
  Lungworms

Ascarids

These live in the intestine. There are two species — the *Toxocara cati* and the *Toxascaris leonina*.

The *Toxocara* lives in the small intestine where it lays eggs which are passed out in the dung. In the damp moist conditions of the outer world, the eggs develop into larvae which become infective. If or when these are swallowed by a cat, they hatch out and migrate through the liver and lungs before returning to the bowel to grow into adult worms. The larval stages can also be transmitted in the mother's milk. With *Toxascaris* there is no such milk-borne infection.

Symptoms

These appear only when the worms are present in large numbers.

The kitten becomes unthrifty, pot-bellied and anaemic (*photo 1*). It develops diarrhoea and may vomit some of the adult worms.

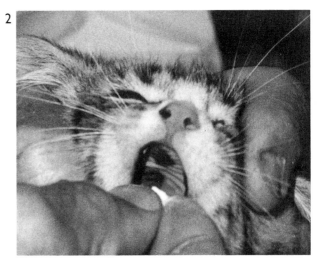

Treatment

Comprises dosing with piperazine — your veterinary surgeon will prescribe the dose and show you how to administer it (*photo 2*). Recovery is rapid.

Prevention

Dose kittens as directed by veterinary surgeon and worm the adults every four to six months, especially if the cat is a hunter.

In breeding catteries *Toxocara cati* can be partially controlled by using concrete runs for the mother and kittens and scrubbing the runs out with hot water and washing soda daily to remove or destroy the *Toxocara* eggs.

Hookworms

Again, two species affect cats — the *Uncinaria stenocephala* and the *Ancylostoma tubaeforme*.

The hookworms live in the small intestine and lay eggs which pass out in the dung. In suitable moist conditions, the eggs hatch into larvae which become infective in seven days.

These infective larvae can penetrate a cat's skin. If they do so or if they are swallowed, they migrate through the lungs to the intestine where they grow into adult worms. They attach themselves to the intestinal lining and suck blood.

Symptoms

Obviously one of the outstanding symptoms of a hookworm infestation is anaemia. This leads to emaciation and general weakness, sometimes with a haemorrhagic diarrhoea. If the larvae have passed through the skin, the emaciated cat will have an itchy dermatitis to complicate the picture.

Treatment

Your veterinary surgeon will prescribe the correct anthelmintic, probably a proprietary one containing a drug called thenium combined with piperazine to destroy any ascarids that may be present as well.

Fortunately, in my experience, severe hookworm infestations are not common. In fact they are extremely rare in Britain and occur mostly in hot climates, e.g., in South America and the Caribbean.

Lungworms

The cat lungworm has the exotic name of *Aelurostrongylus abstrusus*. Like the hookworm, it is not all that commonly diagnosed, though recent surveys have shown that 10-20% of British cats harbour this slender hair-like worm.

Symptoms

Persistent coughing and sneezing leading to pneumonia and pleurisy despite antibiotic therapy.

Treatment

The diagnosis and treatment of lungworms is difficult and very much a job for your veterinary surgeon.

The drug called tetramisole given by the mouth is probably the most effective treatment. All anti-parasitic drugs are constantly being updated and improved.

THE TAPEWORM

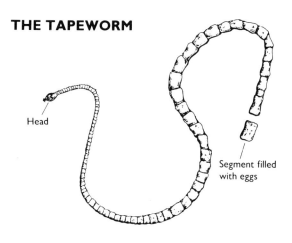

Head

Segment filled with eggs

TAPEWORMS

The tapeworm most often found in the cat is the dog tapeworm called the *Dipylidium caninum* (*see diagram*), though occasionally another one called the *Taenia taeniaeformis* is involved.

Symptoms

Often the only sign of tapeworm infestation is the presence of live segments in the fur around the anus. Affected cats may show a voracious appetite without putting on weight.

Treatment

Two interesting facts have to be borne in mind. Firstly in the life cycle of the *Dipylidium*, the eggs are passed out in the segments and they are then eaten by flea larvae and develop into the infective stage inside the adult flea (*see diagram*). When the flea is swallowed by a cat, the infective larva

THE CAT FLEA

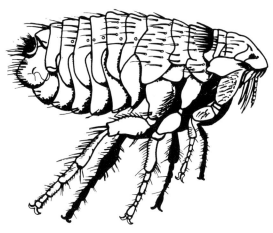

escapes and reaches the intestine to develop into an adult tapeworm.

In the case of the *Taenia*, the infective larvae develop in the livers of mice, rats, and rabbits — all natural prey of the cat.

Dosing with a specific anti-tapeworm drug therefore must be combined with controlling the fleas (if the tapeworm is a *Dipylidium*) or restricting the cat's hunting (if a *Taenia*).

Your veterinary surgeon will be able to identify the tapeworm and advise accordingly. The drugs he will prescribe are much stronger and more effective than those advertised in pet shops. He now has available a powerful injection marketed under the proprietary name of Dronchit.

Prevention
A routine injection every four to six months (*photo 3*).

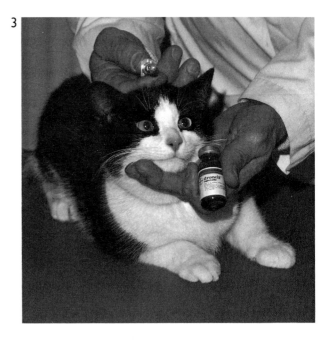

29
The Pharynx and Larynx

Pharyngitis
This means simply inflammation of the pharynx or back of the throat (*photo 1*).

Cause
Most often seen in cats suffering from a certain type of influenza (see page 69) in which case the inflammation can be very severe and painful with ulcers developing in advanced untreated cases.

Pharyngitis may develop secondary to infective gingivitis or pyorrhoea or it may be traumatic, that is, caused by injury from a foreign body.

Symptoms
Loss of appetite. The cat may crouch over a saucer of milk or food as though it wants to drink or eat but can't. It may or may not salivate profusely (*photo 2*).

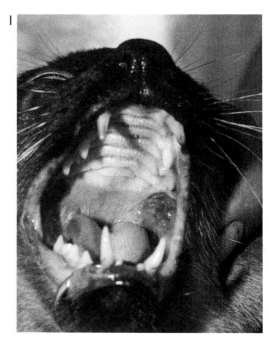

Treatment

Fortunately this condition responds spectacularly to antibiotic injections.

Laryngitis

Inflammation of the larynx or voice box.

Cause

Usually secondary to a respiratory virus infection. The virus damages the lining of the larynx and allows bacteria to grow and develop there.

Symptoms

Difficulty in swallowing and an alteration in the character of the meow. The patient seems to have a pain around the epiglottis and pressure in that region produces distressed coughing (*photo 3*). The body temperature may be raised to 104°F (40°C). (Normal temperature is 101.5°F (38.5°C).

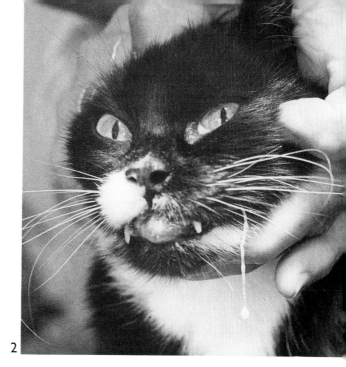

2

Treatment

A five-day course of broad-spectrum antibiotic injections containing cortisone is often necessary. Long-acting injections are available. Oral treatment is difficult and unsatisfactory.

Allergic laryngitis

This can occur as a result of a wasp sting or an insect bite.

Symptoms

The larynx becomes swollen and oedematous (dropsical), and the cat has great difficulty in breathing.

3

Treatment

An urgent visit to your veterinary surgeon. He will inject antihistamine and steroid and may have to do an emergency tracheotomy (i.e., open into the trachea to allow the cat to breathe freely till the laryngeal oedema subsides).

Tumours of the larynx

Seen only occasionally and then mainly in old cats.

Cause

Cancerous growths which develop in the laryngeal wall.

Symptoms

The first sign is a change in the voice and purr. This

is followed by a snoring sound during breathing. The breath may smell foul. When the cat's mouth is forced open there is obvious acute pain.

Treatment

A veterinary surgeon will have to diagnose the condition. Treatment comprises painless euthanasia.

Foreign bodies in the pharynx and larynx

The most common ones encountered in the pharyngeal and laryngeal area are needles, though on several occasions I've had to remove a fish bone. Kittens are the worst offenders — they play with a thread, swallow and find they have to keep swallowing till the needle attached to the thread

51

sticks in the mouth or throat (*photo 4*).

Symptoms
Slobbering, distress and refusal to eat or drink;
coughing and attempts to vomit.

Treatment
An emergency job for your veterinary surgeon.
He may have to X-ray and remove the needle or
bone under a general anaesthetic.

4

30
The Bronchi and the Lungs

THE BRONCHI

The bronchi are the two main branches of the
trachea or windpipe. They extend into each lung
where they ramify to form the lung tissue (*see
diagram*).

Bronchitis
This simply means inflammation of the broncheal
lining. The insides of the bronchi are lined by a
moist ciliated mucous membrane not unlike that
seen in the nasal chambers.

Cause
Usually bacteria which move in after a virus
infection has damaged the mucous membrane.

Symptoms
Coughing and distressed breathing. The
temperature may be up to 104 or 105°F (40 or
40.6°C).

Treatment
Your veterinary surgeon will confirm the diagnosis
by using his stethoscope and will prescribe broad-
spectrum antibiotics by injection and by the mouth.
Recovery is often spectacular. Personally I use an

THE LUNGS

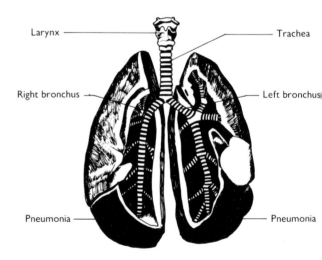

Larynx — Trachea — Right bronchus — Left bronchus — Pneumonia — Pneumonia

injection containing a mixture of broad spectrum
antibiotic, cortisone and antihistamine to allay the
irritation and inflammation quickly.

THE LUNGS

The cat's lungs, like those of all other animals, are
similar to sponges, i.e., made up of masses of

1　The cat's whiskers.　▲

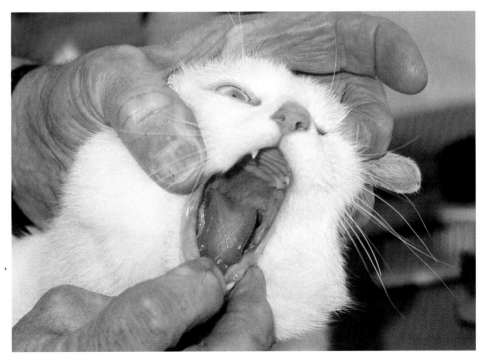

2　The cat's tongue
showing its
roughness and
powerful papillae.　▶

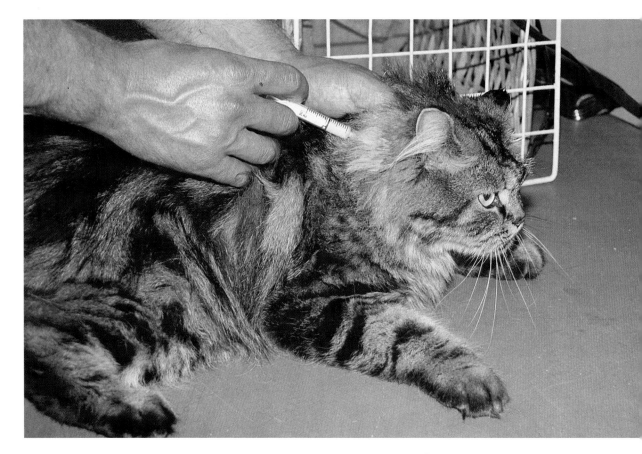

3   Injecting cat with tranquiliser before a long car journey. ▲

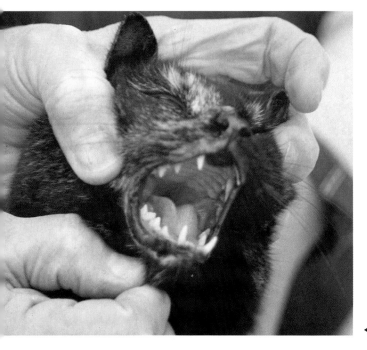

◀ 4   The typical teeth of a carnivore.

◀ 5   Coming out of the cat door.

6   A useful cat basket plus the
best type of feeding bowls. ▶

7   **The kitten settling down in a new environment.** ▲

8   **Grooming the cat.** ▼

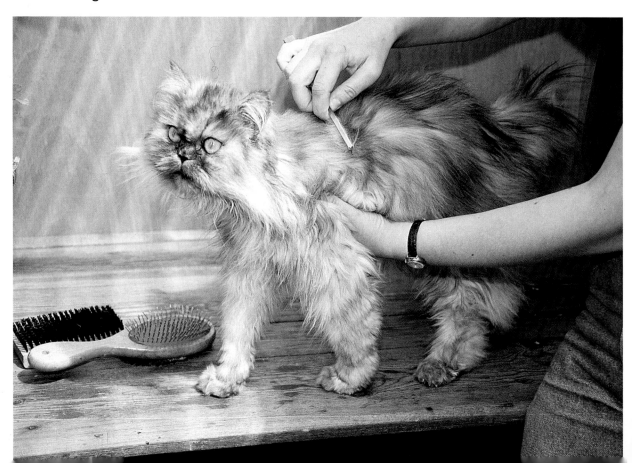

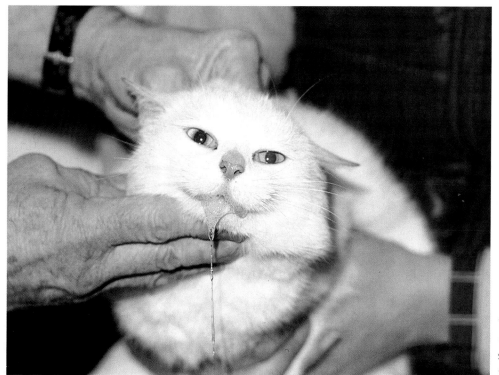

◀ **9** Dribbling associated with sickness or bad teeth.

10 A female cat in season. ▶

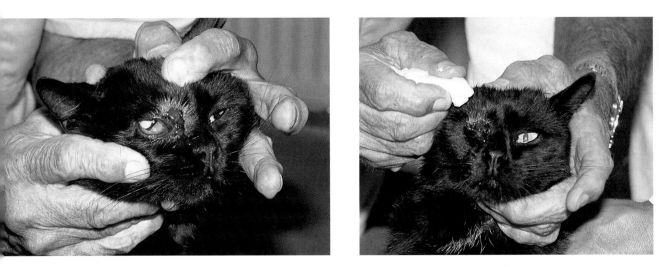

11　A damaged eye. ▲　　　Bathing eye with saline using cotton wool. ▲

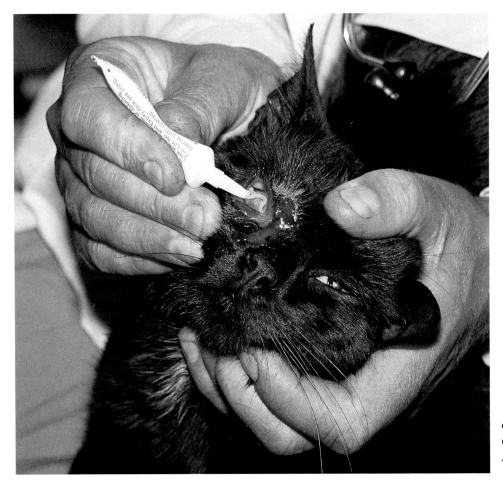

12　Inserting
ointment into
damaged eye.

◄

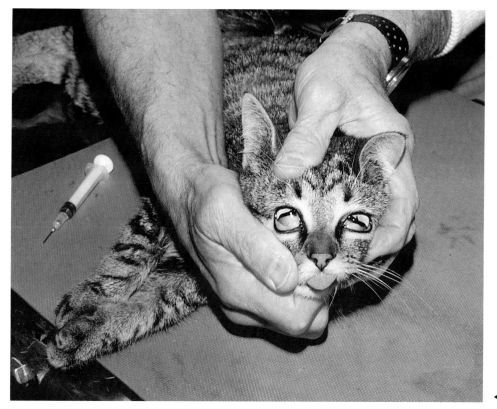

13 **A cat with** ◀ haw.

14 **A dirty ear — possibly otodectic mange.** ▼

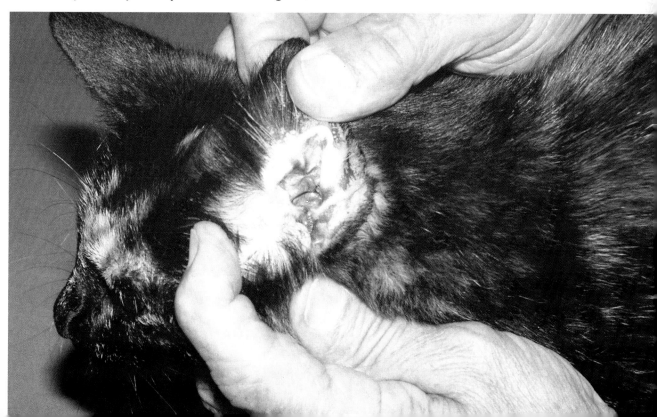

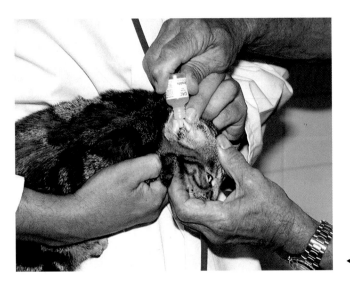

15 Dressing cat's ear for otodectic mange.

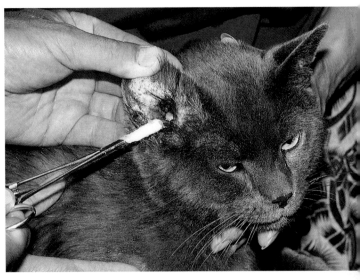

16 Cleaning out an infected ear. This job should only be done by the veterinary surgeon because of the risk of damaging the delicate ear lining.

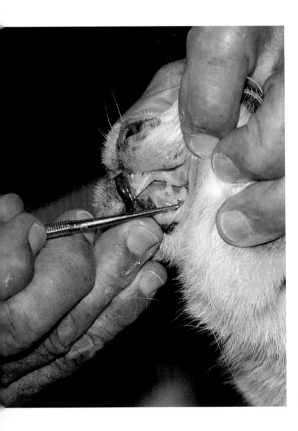

17 Scaling the teeth (removing the tartar).

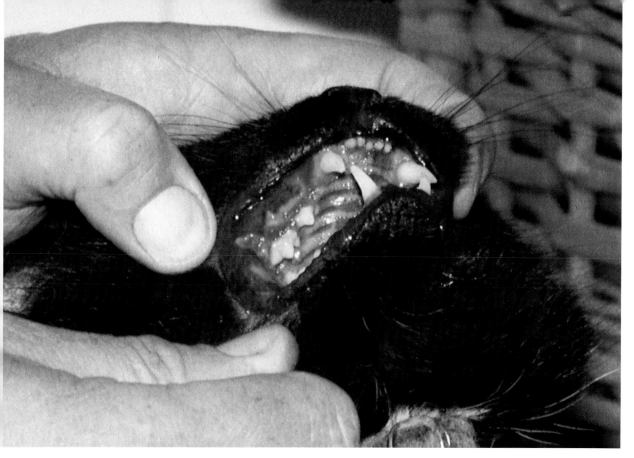

18   Gingivitis — acute inflammation of the gums. ▲

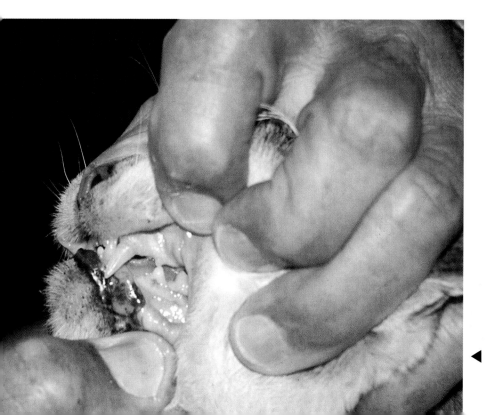

19   During all routine examinations the veterinary surgeon will check the teeth for plaque and/or ◀ tartar.

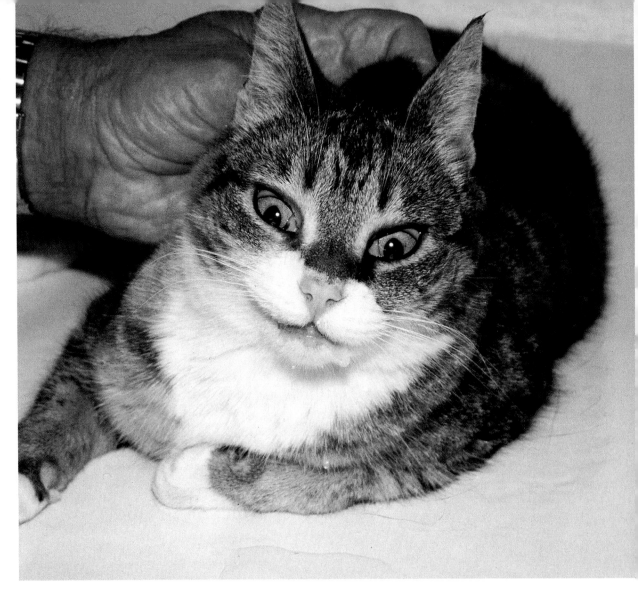

▲ 20   An apparently healthy cat suddenly dribbling at the mouth. A bad tooth? More likely a piece of bone or other foreign body lodged in the mouth. In this instance a piece of bone.

◄ 21   The discharging eyes of a cat with cat flu.

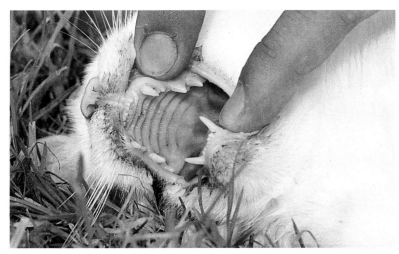

◀ **22   The typical mouth membranes found in organophosphorous poisoning.**

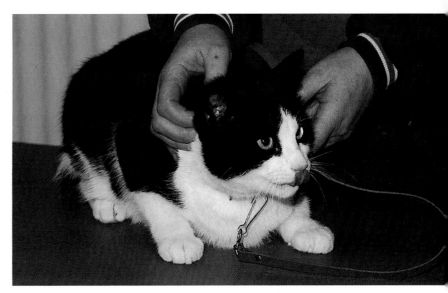

23   Dilated pupils — typical of Key-Gaskell syndrome. ▶

24   An old cat with arthritis that causes difficulty in standing and ◀ walking.

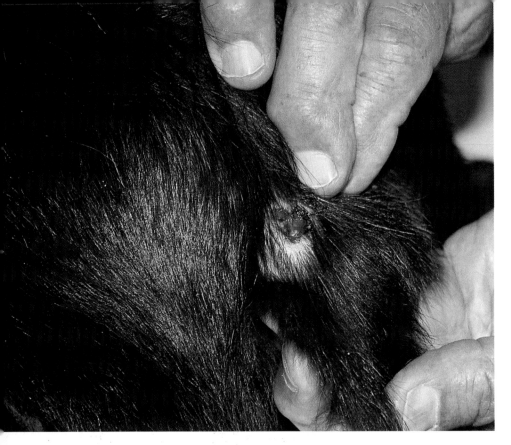

25 An abscess formation at the root of the cat's tail, secondary to ▲
a dog or cat bite.

26 An abscess on the cheek, secondary to a rat bite. ▼

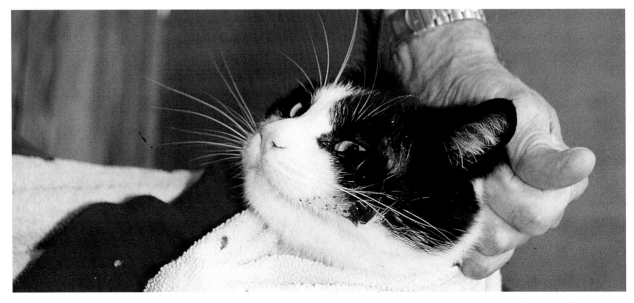

minute spaces or sacs. They are divided into well-marked zones or lobes — four in the right lung and three in the left.

Pneumonia
Pneumonia simply means lack of air or oxygen.

Cause
An acute bacterial invasion of the minute air sacs. Multiplication of the bacteria produces inflammation which fills up the air sacs and cuts down the amount of the cat's available oxygen. Virus infections and/or lungworms may trigger off the bacteria.

Symptoms
Difficult breathing with a distinct expiratory grunt and an occasional cough. The appetite is lost: small wonder since the temperature usually rises to around 105°F (40.6°C). Needless to say, the cat will be depressed and loathe to move around.

Treatment
See your veterinary surgeon immediately; he will diagnose the cause and treat the condition with powerful broad-spectrum antibiotics. If he suspects lungworms, he will eliminate these. He will also advise on nursing the patient — a constant warm temperature in an environment containing plenty of fresh air but no draughts, etc.

Pleurisy
Inflammation of the pleura, the fine membrane which lines the chest and is reflected over both lungs. It is a very serious condition in cats.

Cause
Usually associated with or secondary to pneumonia. Bacteria invade the pleural sac (i.e. the space between the chest pleura and the reflected lung pleura), filling it up with inflammatory exudate — thick pus-like fluid.

Symptoms
The pressure of the fluid in the pleural sac causes partial or complete collapse of the affected lung. Auscultation of the affected area with a stethoscope reveals sandpaper-like rales and fluid noises (photo 1).
  Breathing is distressed; the patient is completely off food and runs a high temperature.

Treatment
Very much a job for a skilled veterinarian. The fluid has to be drained out through a special cannula under a general anaesthetic. At the same time an intensive antibiotic therapy is necessary. I have treated many but saved only a few.

OTHER PLEURAL CONDITIONS

Hydrothorax
This occurs when the thorax or chest cavity fills up with a watery, serum-type fluid.

Cause
Hydrothorax is a symptom of one of two very serious conditions — cancer of the lymph glands between the lungs (lymphosarcoma) or congestive heart failure.

Symptoms
Acutely distressed breathing with the cat poking its head forward in a desperate effort to inhale sufficient oxygen to keep the body alive. The membranes of the mouth and eye become cyanosed (purple).

Treatment
Prompt and painless euthanasia.

Pneumothorax
In this air collects inside the thorax.

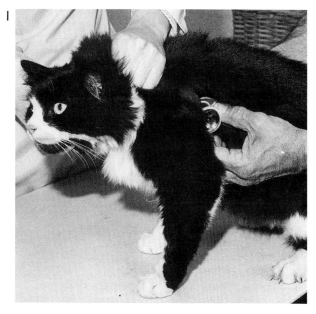

Cause
A penetrating chest wound caused either by buckshot or by being hit by a vehicle.

Symptoms
Acute and progressive respiratory distress.

Treatment
Urgent attention by your veterinary surgeon who will treat the case as an emergency. He will anaesthetise the cat with closed-circuit anaesthesia to keep the lungs functioning while he withdraws the air from the upper part of the chest and repairs the punctured wound in the thoracic wall.

Fortunately, pneumothorax in the cat seldom occurs — I've seen only two cases in the last fifteen years.

Tuberculosis and cancer of the lungs
Fortunately, both of these are extremely rare in the cat's lungs.

Tuberculosis, now rapidly disappearing owing to the control of cattle TB, attacks the throat glands, the intestine or the liver.

Cancer attacks the lymph glands, intestinal tract or the reproductive organs mainly.

Treatment
When either of these diseases is diagnosed, immediate euthanasia is indicated.

31
The Oesophagus

This is the foodpipe extending from the pharynx to the stomach (see *diagram on page 55*).

Oesophageal obstruction
Cause
A small bone, like a vertebra, hastily swallowed and stuck usually three-quarters of the way down; a portion of a plastic toy; or a small sewing needle.

In kittens a congenital anatomical defect called a persistent right aortic arch causes an obstruction about half-way down.

Symptoms
Vomiting within seconds of eating solid food. The cat or kitten seems willing and keen to eat but vomits the food literally straight back.

Treatment
X-ray and surgical removal of the foreign body by your veterinary surgeon.

Competent surgery can also correct the effect of the congenital persistent aortic arch.

Infection of the oesophagus by viruses or bacteria
This can occur as a spread of infection from the respiratory organs, usually the pharynx or larynx.

Symptoms
Not unlike those of obstruction — difficulty in swallowing food followed by vomiting.

Treatment
The diagnosis and treatment of this requires the considerable skill of a veterinary surgeon.

Cancer of the oesophagus
The oesophageal wall is one of the sites where a malignant growth is liable to develop, especially in an older cat.

Symptoms
Similar to those caused by a foreign body

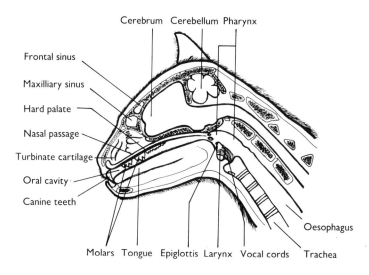

Cerebrum Cerebellum Pharynx

Frontal sinus

Maxilliary sinus

Hard palate

Nasal passage

Turbinate cartilage

Oral cavity

Canine teeth

Molars Tongue Epiglottis Larynx Vocal cords Trachea

Oesophagus

obstruction. Only an X-ray or exploratory surgery
will confirm the growth's presence.

Treatment
Euthanasia.

32
The Stomach

The stomach of a cat is relatively large and
extremely tough. It is adapted to cope in the wild
state with occasional gorgings as and when the wild
cat finds suitable prey.

Gastritis
Means inflammation of the mucous membrane or
lining of the stomach.

Cause
Usually some irritant licked from the coat during
the cat's daily toilet. The hairs themselves when
swallowed can produce a mild gastritis. Bacterial
gastritis can occur in food poisoning.

Symptoms
Vomiting and abdominal pain or discomfort evinced
by the patient tucking his abdomen up in a
crouched position on the coldest surface he can
find. Excessive drinking is followed by vomiting.

Treatment
This depends on the cause. If there is no sign of
irritant on the fur, I administer a tranquilliser to
stop the vomiting and follow up with a gastric
sedative and antibiotic, both given by the mouth
and repeated in twelve hours. No food is given for
twenty-four hours, then small quantities four times
daily.
  At the same time, I insist on twice daily
grooming for at least a week: this not only
removes the excess hair but it makes the cat feel
better.

Foreign bodies in the stomach
Foreign bodies such as bones, pieces of plastic,

needles, etc. don't usually cause trouble until they enter the intestine.

Symptoms
Usually non-existent. The story is that the animal has been seen to swallow the offending object.

Treatment
X-ray followed by immediate surgical removal. I always think prevention is better than cure and it seems stupid to wait until there is an intestinal obstruction.

Fur ball
In the stomach this merely causes a mild gastritis which often produces the reflex vomiting necessary to get rid of the fur ball. In other words, nature usually takes care of gastric fur balls, bringing them up approximately every fortnight.

Just occasionally they are not vomited back, and as they get bigger, the cat goes off its feed and loses condition. In such cases, the ball has to be removed surgically.

Prevention is by frequent grooming.

Pyloric stenosis
This occurs when the opening from the stomach into the duodenum, called the pylorus, is constricted and doesn't function properly.

Cause
Most cases I've come across have been congenital and permanent, though I have seen several develop later in life.

Symptoms
The cat is always hungry but within a few minutes of eating he vomits it back forcibly — what we call projectile vomiting. Needless to say, the cat rapidly loses condition.

Treatment
Very much one for your veterinary surgeon. He will confirm the diagnosis by a barium X-ray and will probably operate.

The operation comprises cutting through the muscular ring around the pylorus and is usually spectacularly successful.

33
The Liver

The liver is the factory of the body where all the simple products of digestion are elaborated before being transported to the various parts of the anatomy. Obviously, therefore, any disease of the liver is very serious.

Hepatitis
Inflammation of the liver.

Cause
Damage caused by the ingestion of toxic substances (see Steatitis, page 76) or by the invasion of the liver tissue by bacteria or viruses. The toxic substances may be licked from the coat.

Symptoms
Acute depression with the membranes of the eye and mouth coloured bright yellow or orange. In steatitis the subcutaneous fat of the belly is clearly jaundiced.

Diarrhoea or acute constipation and occasionally nervous symptoms, namely excitability and muscle tremors.

If the hepatitis becomes chronic, the cat develops ascites (fluid in the abdomen).

Treatment
An immediate visit to your veterinary surgeon. He will first of all remove or treat the cause, then will probably put the cat on glucose, steroids and amino acid, plus a completely fat-free diet for some time if or when the cat starts to eat.

With chronic cases the best treatment is euthanasia.

34
The Intestines

Enteritis

Inflammation of the lining of the bowel. In the cat this is mostly seen in conjunction with gastritis. In such cases the diagnosis is gastro-enteritis.

Cause

Enteritis can be due to viral or bacterial invasion of the mucous membrane or to one of many other factors such as feed changes, poisons, parasites (ascarids and hookworms), etc.

Symptoms

Diarrhoea which may be acute, chronic or haemorrhagic (blood-stained).

Treatment

First-aid treatment consists of withholding solid food, but the sooner an enteritis case is examined by a veterinary surgeon the better. He will prescribe the correct treatment only after diagnosing the precise cause (*photo 1*).

Prevention

The most dangerous type of enteritis is the viral feline enteritis, and all kittens should be vaccinated against this at ten to twelve weeks and every year thereafter (see Feline enteritis, page 68).

Foreign bodies in the intestine
Cause

Any obstruction from a fur ball to a needle, child's toy or impacted bone — I've even removed pieces of string and plastic.

Symptoms

The outstanding sign is vomiting within an hour or two of eating. This may persist for several days; the cat is constipated and becomes morose and extremely unhappy. It may show signs of acute abdominal pain, especially if peritonitis develops. The same train of symptoms can be seen when the rectum is impacted with solid faeces.

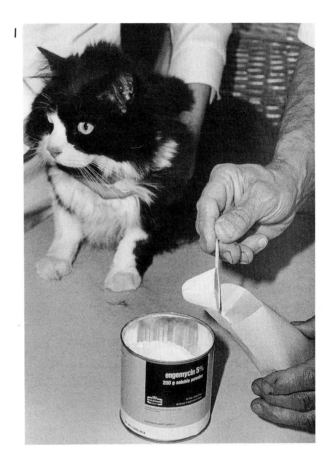

1

Treatment

X-ray and surgical removal as soon as possible. Undue delay can lead to fatal peritonitis.

The surgeon will endeavour to remove the offending impaction through a piece of healthy bowel wall so that the cat will recover and heal up more quickly.

After-treatment comprises at least three days on liquids followed by a week on soft, easily digested foods.

The success rate, provided the operation can be done in reasonable time, is almost one hundred per cent.

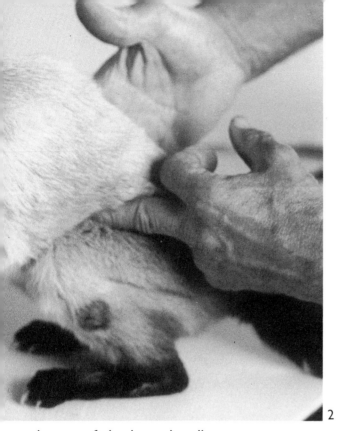

the intestine within itself, causing obstruction.

Cause
Often obscure. The problem is most likely to occur when the cat is suffering from enteritis.

Symptoms
Off food; vomiting and abdominal pain.

Treatment
Immediate surgery. The veterinary surgeon will probably remove the affected part and resect the intestine.

Impaction of the anal glands
On either side of and slightly below the anus are two small glands called the anal glands.

During defaecation (the passing of the motion) the contents of the glands, thought to have some lubricating effect, are passed through small ducts to the anus. Occasionally, these glands become impacted, though not by any means as frequently as they do in dogs.

2

Atony of the bowel wall
This occurs mainly in old cats.

Cause
Senile loss of tone of the intestinal wall in the lower part of the colon and in the rectum.

Symptoms
Acute constipation leading to the typical signs of intestinal obstruction — that is, vomiting followed by general depression. The cat may repeatedly squat in an effort to pass the dry faecal mass.

Usually the veterinary surgeon can feel the hard mass in the abdomen (*photo 2*).

Treatment
Confirmatory diagnosis by X-ray followed by surgical removal of the mass. Liquid paraffin in the mouth and by enema are rarely successful in an acute impaction.

Prevention
It is a good idea to add approximately ½ teaspoonful of liquid paraffin to every feed given to a cat aged over twelve years.

Intussusception
Intussusception means a folding or telescoping of

3

Symptoms
Repeated sitting down and licking at the rear end (*photo 3*). Sometimes the impacted glands have become infected with a resultant abscess formation.

Treatment
The veterinary surgeon will express the anal glands. If an abscess is present, he may lance it. In either case it is a professional task.

58

35
The Heart and the Blood Vessels

The cat has a comparatively small but exceptionally strong heart (*see diagram*).

As in all animals the heart is a powerful pump comprising the strongest muscle in the body.

It is surrounded by a serous membrane or sac called the pericardium, which under normal circumstances contains a small quantity of lubricating fluid called the pericardial fluid.

The heart comprises two lower chambers with extremely thick walls (the right and left ventricles) and two upper cavities with slightly thinner walls (the right and left auricles). The left-sided chambers are both larger than the right.

As the blood passes round the body, it collects carbon dioxide from the various tissues and this is carried by the veins to the right auricle.

It then passes through a valved opening into the right ventricle and from there the thick walls pump it to the lungs through the pulmonary artery.

In the lungs the carbon dioxide is expelled as the cat breathes out, and oxygen takes its place as the cat breathes in. The oxygenated blood is then carried back to the left auricle by the pulmonary vein. From there it passes through another valved opening into the left ventricle — the most efficient pumping chamber ever created.

THE HEART

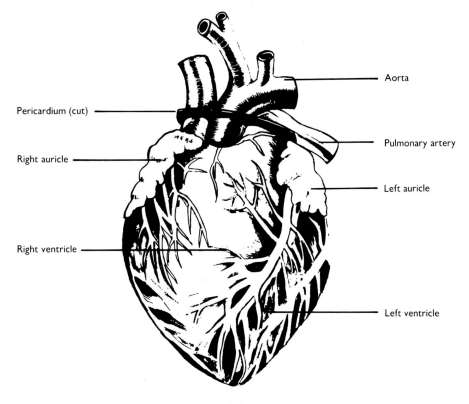

Pericardium (cut)

Right auricle

Right ventricle

Aorta

Pulmonary artery

Left auricle

Left ventricle

The left ventricle pumps the oxygenated blood through the arteries round the entire body (*see diagram*).

The process is continuous, starting when the kitten is in the embryo state within the mother's womb and stopping only when the cat dies.

Heart disease

The cat is extremely fortunate in that it rarely suffers from heart disease.

Valvular incompetence, cardiac hypertension and arteriosclerosis — all comparatively common in the dog and in humans — are seen only in the late stages of senility as part of the natural dying process. All combine to make the end rapid and comparatively painless.

Thrombosis in the main artery supplying the hind legs has occasionally been recorded. It causes pain and paralysis.

I have seen an occasional inter-bred kitten with a congenital valvular incompetence. In oriental breeds, heart defects may be hereditary; these can be detected by chest X-rays after injecting a special radio-opaque material intravenously.

But, all in all, heart problems in cats are so rare that for the purposes of this book they can be disregarded.

BLOOD CIRCULATION

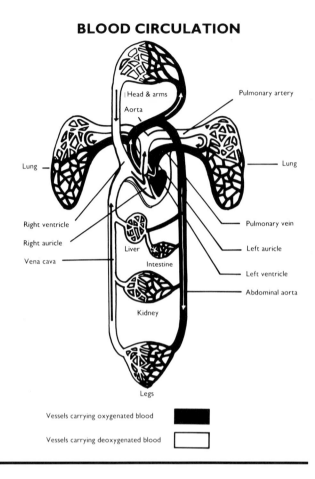

Head & arms
Aorta
Pulmonary artery
Lung
Lung
Right ventricle
Pulmonary vein
Right auricle
Liver
Left auricle
Vena cava
Intestine
Left ventricle
Abdominal aorta
Kidney
Legs

Vessels carrying oxygenated blood
Vessels carrying deoxygenated blood

36
The Urinary System: The Bladder

The urinary system comprises the two kidneys, two ureters, the bladder and the urethra.

In my experience of cat practice, bladder troubles are the most common.

Cystitis
Inflammation of the bladder.

Cause
Usually a bacterial infection, though I have seen it flare up for no apparent reason where the urine has proved to be sterile on laboratory culture.

Cystitis can be an early sign of stones or of sand in the bladder.

Symptoms
Repeated and continual attempts to urinate, with small strong-smelling drops only passed often bloodstained.

The affected cat may spend several frustrating hours digging hole after hole in the garden.

If untreated, the temperature may rise to around 103 or 104°F (39 or 40°C) and the cat drinks excessively and walks stiffly.

Treatment
Where the condition is not complicated by stones

or sand, broad-spectrum antibiotics and special urinary sulphonamides given by the mouth and/or by injection effect a rapid cure.

If symptoms persist, calculi should be suspected.

Calculi

Calculi, which are stones in the bladder, are nothing like as common as in dogs and are seen mostly in the female cat.

Cause

Obscure, probably associated with the alkaline content of the drinking water and diet.

Symptoms

Identical to those seen in cystitis, with the blood-stained urine more copious and apparent. Any cystitis which doesn't respond to treatment is suspect.

Treatment

X-ray and surgical removal.

Prevention

The stones can be analysed and your veterinary surgeon will then advise on preventative therapy. He may suggest a special low-ash diet containing acid sodium phosphate.

Bladder sand and crystals

Nowadays gritty material in the bladder causes a great deal more trouble than calculi and appears to be an ever-increasing problem.

Cause

Unknown; personally, I suspect a virus infection.

Dry-feeding appears to predispose to this condition: certainly the majority of cases I treat have been dry-fed. This would seem to indicate that any fluid shortage predisposes to the flare up.

What happens is that small, sand-like crystals or sebulous plugs of a substance called struvite are precipitated out of the urine and block up the urethra.

Symptoms

The cat goes off its feed and squats continually in an effort to pass urine. The owner often thinks the squatting is due to constipation.

If not treated rapidly, the cat becomes really ill, moaning in pain during its repeated attempts at micturition and often vomiting.

Treatment

It is absolutely vital that suspect cases should be taken to a veterinary surgeon at once. The earlier the surgeon sees the cat, the better chance it will have. Delays lead to bladder infection, haemorrhage and general uraemia — all serious complications.

Emergency surgery is performed, the bladder cleaned out of all material and the urethral obstruction removed if at all possible. It may be necessary to by-pass the obstruction and pass the clear portion of the urethra directly through the abdominal wall.

The death rate is high if the owner delays in having the patient attended to.

Prevention

Avoid dry feeding. Add plenty of water to each feed — mash in at least half a cupful.

The struvite is composed of magnesium ammonium phosphate so it is wise, after an attack, to avoid high magnesium foods like fish and meat and put on a diet of milk, eggs, carrots and tinned luncheon meat. Several proprietary tinned cat foods are low in magnesium.

Such precautions in the main apply only to known struvite suffers.

With the average cat an avoidance of all dry food is usually the only precaution necessary.

Atony of the bladder

This means loss of tone in the bladder muscle which leads to difficulty in urinating.

Cause

Usually a complication of excessive distension due to bladder sand or calculi, but it may be due to an injury — a kick or being hit by a car — or merely old age.

Symptoms

Distension of the bladder and persistent uncontrolled dribbling.

Treatment

Very much a matter for your veterinary surgeon. He will demonstrate and instruct how to empty the bladder by careful pressure on the abdomen (*photo 1*) and will prescribe broad spectrum antibiotics or urinary sulphonamides to prevent bladder infection until normal tone is recovered.

Treatment of bladder atony requires great

patience from the owner and full cooperation with the veterinary surgeon.

The cat's fur around the urethral oriface will have to be washed carefully every day with warm water and mild non-irritant soap.

Spraying

The vast majority of cats are instinctively clean animals and as domestic pets will rarely foul the home. If or when the odd one sins in this respect, there is usually an underlying cause. Though difficult to cure, the habit of spraying can be treated with a fair chance of success.

Cause

Hormonal
'Spraying' or urine marking is linked with sexual behaviour and is most common in tom cats. A small proportion of females may also spray due to hormonal upsets.

Psychological
Jealousy may be caused by there being more than one cat in the house or by a dog or baby being added to the family. It may be triggered off by the arrival of another cat in the neighbourhood or by the frustration and stress caused by irregular feeding times.

Treatment

Castration of tom cats may cure up to 90 per cent of cases. Where this fails or where the female is the culprit, a course of female hormone, prescribed by your veterinary surgeon, may work spectacularly. The hormones prescribed are synthetic and are marketed under the names of ovarid and perlutex.

If hormonal therapy is unsuccessful, possible psychological factors should be investigated in consultation with your veterinary surgeon.

Other suggested remedies are:

Scrubbing the site of the spraying with hot water, soda and bleach, then placing the food dish on the spot.

Covering the spraying area with tin or aluminium foil. The high-pitched noise of the spraying on the foil has been known to effect a permanent cure.

37
The Urinary System: The Kidneys

The kidneys are complex and delicate in structure and, next to the heart, are probably the most important organs in the body.

Their chief function is to filter the waste products from the blood.

Nephritis

Inflammation of the kidneys. Acute nephritis in the cat is rare. The type usually seen occurs in old cats and is called chronic interstitial nephritis.

Cause

A bacterial infection may trigger it off, but the main cause appears to be senility, since any apparent recovery is mostly temporary.

Symptoms

Gradual wasting and excessive thirst. If you run the hand along the patient's spine, the emaciated frame can be felt through a sparse staring coat (*photo 1*).

If you pick the cat up, it will seem as light as a feather.

The appetite is capricious and the breath may smell foul. Ulcers often appear in the mouth.

The veterinary surgeon will require a urine sample for testing.

Treatment

In the early stages, there is some response to the oral administration of broad-spectrum antibiotics, but as the condition progresses, euthanasia should be considered. Many times I have noticed a tendency for a chronic kidney case to hide itself away. It is much more humane to put such cases to sleep rather than have them disappear to die in solitary misery.

Kidney calculi

These are rare in the cat. In fact in fifty years of vetting I have never seen a kidney calculus in a cat X-ray.

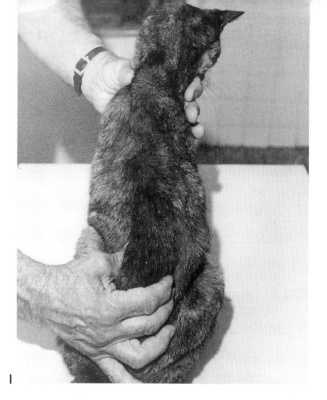

1

38
The Genital System

The male reproductive system comprises the testicles, spermatic cord, seminal vesicles, prostate gland and penis. The testicles are enclosed by the scrotum and the penis is protected by the prepuce.

Veterinary problems in the male genital system in my experience are limited to the odd neoplasm (see Tumours, page 67).

The female reproductive system is made up of the ovaries, oviducts or fallopian tubes, the uterus, vagina, vulva and mammary glands.

The parts of the female reproductive tract which give the most trouble are the uterus, mammary glands and the vagina.

THE UTERUS

Metritis

Inflammation of the uterine lining. Obviously this occurs only in entire queens.

Cause

Dead kittens or retention of an afterbirth.

Symptoms

A foul smelling discharge after kitting (*photo 1*). The queen is off food, runs a temperature of up to 105°F (40.6°C) and goes off her milk.

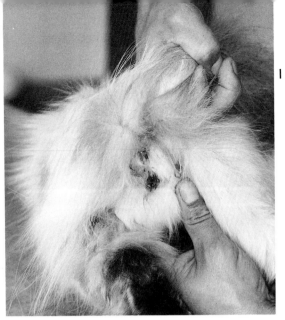

1

Treatment
An immediate visit to a veterinary surgeon. If treated early, the condition responds very well to antibiotic injections.

Pyometra
The accumulation of pus in the uterus.

Cause
A bacterial infection which may be secondary to an abortion but which frequently flares up in ageing queens which have not produced a litter. Since the majority of female pets have had their uteri removed during spaying, the condition is comparatively uncommon.

Symptoms
The earliest sign is excess thirst. There may or may not be a vaginal discharge, but the abdomen is enlarged and a veterinary surgeon will be able to palpate (feel) an enlarged uterus (*photo 2*).
   If neglected, the patient will start to vomit.

Treatment
An immediate ovario-hysterectomy. Caught reasonably early, the cat will recover. If vomiting has set in, its chances are considerably reduced.
   The golden rule with a queen, therefore, is to consult your veterinary surgeon if or when she starts to drink excessively.

2

THE VAGINA

The passage leading from the vulva to the cervix or entrance to the uterus.

Vaginitis
Cause
Trauma from excessive activities of a tom.

Symptoms
Repeated squatting as though trying to urinate, a bloody mucoid or pus-like discharge and persistent licking at the vulva (*photo 3*).

Treatment
This condition can soon be cleared up by local and parenteral antibiotic therapy, so get a suspect case to your veterinary surgeon as early as possible.

3

The Vulva

This is the external opening of the female genital system.

Vulvitis

Cause

As in vaginitis. A severe vulvitis can result also from persistent licking in bladder or kidney troubles.

Treatment

Best left to your veterinary surgeon to diagnose the cause. If due to the trauma of intercourse, local applications of cortisone cream will soon clear it up.

The Mammary Glands

The mammary glands extend in pairs along the floor of the abdomen.

During pregnancy or false pregnancy they swell up, and following the birth of the kittens, they produce the milk to rear them.

Mastitis

Inflammation of the mammary glands. Seen in the breeding queen. It can be acute or chronic (*photo 4*).

Cause

Bacterial infection triggered off by excessive sucking.

Retention of milk following loss of the kittens is another common cause.

Any scratch or wound can allow the bacteria to flare up.

Symptoms

In the acute form, the queen goes off her food and runs a high temperature (105°F/40.6°C). The affected teats are hot, swollen and painful. If the queen is suckling kittens, they will rapidly suffer.

In the chronic form, one or two teats only may be affected and the milk from them is watery and clotted.

Treatment

A rapid response is usually obtained from antibiotic injections, so get your queen to a veterinary surgeon immediately you suspect mastitis: otherwise you may lose the litter.

If the kittens are old enough, wean them immediately. If not, hand-feed them until the queen is better.

4
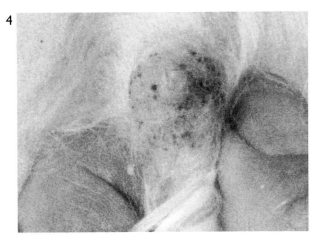

39
Hernias (Ruptures)

Four types of hernias are seen in cats:

    Inguinal   Scrotal
    Umbilical   Diaphragmatic

Inguinal hernia

Cause

Tearing or stretching of the inguinal canal which

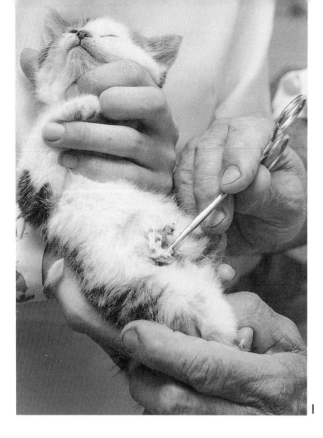

Scrotal hernia
Cause
Excess strain or accident. The bowel descends into the scrotum or sac containing the testicles. Rare in the cat — I've seen only three in fifty years.

Treatment
Immediate operation with possible necessity of simultaneous castration.

Diaphragmatic hernia
Cause
Chiefly road accidents, though the odd congenital case has been recorded.

Symptoms
The abdominal contents spill through the diaphragm into the chest cavity (*see diagram*). The cat breathes heavily as though suffering from pneumonia. Temperature is normal but peculiar sounds are heard in the chest.

Respiratory distress increases markedly if you suspend the cat by the hind legs.

X-ray confirms the diagnosis.

allows the bowel, enclosed in a peritoneal sac, to descend inside the canal. Apparently there can be an hereditary predisposition to this.

Symptoms
A soft swelling in the groin on either or both sides. The swelling varies in size and disappears on pressure.

Treatment
I always advise immediate surgery because of the danger of strangulation.

Umbilical hernia
Cause
Navel rupture or incomplete closure of the umbilicus or navel with the kitten is born (*photo 1*).

Symptoms
Usually only a small swelling, very occasionally a large one.

Treatment
The small ones contain only fat and are best left alone. Operation on the larger ones should be left to the discretion of your veterinary surgeon.

DIAPHRAGMATIC HERNIA

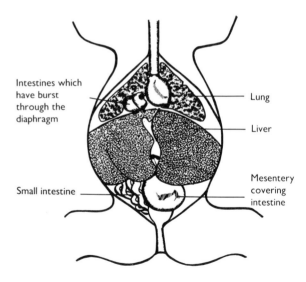

Intestines which have burst through the diaphragm

Lung

Liver

Small intestine

Mesentery covering intestine

Treatment
An immediate emergency operation which requires special anaesthesia technique and all the skill of the veterinary surgeon.

40
Tumours

The technical term for a tumour is neoplasm, which may be benign or malignant.

The benign type grows slowly without spreading. The malignant grows rapidly, infiltrates into surrounding tissues and spreads to other parts of the body via the bloodstream.

The great majority of cat tumours are malignant, so any suspect swelling or lump on a cat should be investigated by a veterinary surgeon immediately (*photo 1*).

Cat cancer can occur in the mouth, pharynx, larynx, oesophagus, intestines, lymphatic glands, the skin, the bones and in the female reproductive system. In the male genitals, the testicles are the most vulnerable.

The two commonest types in my experience are mammary tumours and leukaemia (see Virus Diseases).

Mammary tumours
Symptoms
A hard lump under one or several of the teats (*photo 2*).

Treatment
Immediate surgical removal by the veterinary surgeon.

Prognosis
Reasonable if caught early.

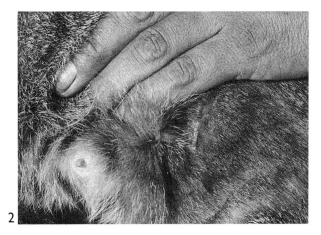

1

2

41
Virus Diseases

Feline leukaemia
Leukaemia is a cancer of the white blood corpuscles. The malignancy causes excessive multiplication of the white cells and this in turn leads to swelling of the lymphatic glands and the spleen (where the white cells are normally

produced). If the patient survives long enough, other organs become affected.

Cause
A virus called FLV, similar to the virus causing leukaemia in poultry.

Mode of spread
Some cats act as carriers of the virus without showing symptoms. For example, there is evidence that the virus is transmitted by some pregnant mothers to the kittens before or immediately after birth.

In an active case, all secretions and excretions contain the virus, which spreads by direct contact or by a cat eating infected material.

Symptoms
A persistent fever ruins the cat's appetite. Inevitably progressive weakness, wasting and anaemia follow. The spine becomes more prominent (*photo 1*). The lymphatic glands become swollen and hard, the most obvious being those in front of the shoulder and at the back of the hind leg.

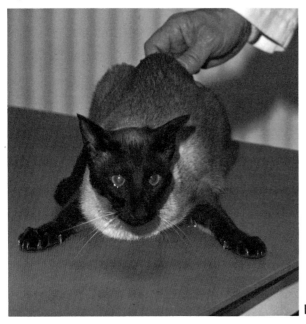
1

An enlarged spleen causes intermittent vomiting and diarrhoea. Later, damaged kidneys produce renal failure and, if the cat lives long enough, chest complications develop.

Kittens infected in utero (i.e. inside the mother) usually show signs of brain damage.

Diagnosis
This is confirmed by a blood test. Because of the carrier danger, British licensed breed stock have to be regularly tested.

The two conditions most likely to be confused with feline leukaemia are feline infectious anaemia and feline infectious peritonitis.

Treatment
There is none. Some workers claim a 10 per cent natural recovery but in my experience the mortality rate is 100 per cent and therefore I recommend immediate euthanasia once the diagnosis is definitely established.

Feline infectious enteritis
Panleucopaenia is without doubt the most dangerous killer disease of cats (*photo 2*).

2
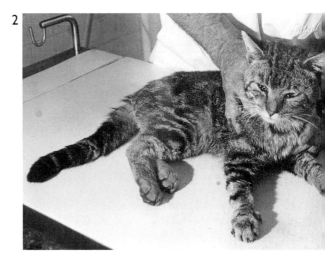

Cause
A virus affecting only members of the cat family. The virus lowers the cat's resistance by destroying a percentage of the white blood corpuscles.

Symptoms
The symptoms are seen mostly in young cats and appear between four and ten days after the virus is picked up.

An initial high fever (105° or 106°F/40.6° or 41.1°C) is followed by vomiting and rapid dehydration. The vomit comprises frothy, yellow-stained fluid.

The cat refuses to eat but will often sit crouched over the drinking bowl or seek out a cold surface to lie on.

Diarrhoea does not develop unless the patient survives for a few days.

Some adult cats can carry the virus and a carrier mother may transmit it to the kittens before birth. When this happens the kittens' brains are affected producing a condition called cerebellar ataxia. Symptoms appear at two to three months. The kittens show a high stepping gait and stagger or fall about when they try to walk (*photo 3*).

Treatment
Ataxia kittens should be put to sleep.

The panleucopaenia patients sometimes respond to broad-spectrum antibiotics and fluid therapy, but since this is the one cat disease that can be controlled by vaccination, prevention is infinitely preferable to treatment.

Prevention
All kittens should be vaccinated against feline enteritis at the age of ten to twelve weeks and should have a regular booster vaccination every year (*photo 4*).

The vaccines are first-class and almost 100 per cent effective.

If taking a cat to a show, make sure it is fully protected. If a kitten, innoculate it one month before the show.

Cat influenza
Throughout the years, I have observed two different types of cat influenza, both of which fortunately respond well to treatment.

Cause
It is known that two distinct viruses are involved. One is called the herpes virus and the other, the *Feline picornavirus (Feline calicivirus)*.

Symptoms
Type A
This is known as feline viral rhinotracheitis, and in my opinion it is produced by the herpes virus. There is a rise in temperature to around 103° – 104°F (39.4° – 40°C) which persists for three to four days and then returns to normal. During that time the cat is dull and off food.

Marked secondary respiratory symptoms now start — sneezing, coughing and a watery discharge from the eyes and nose (*photo 5 and colour plate 20*). This discharge rapidly changes into pus and the eyelids may become gummed up.

3

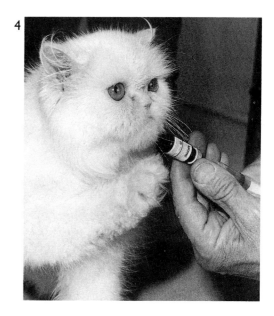

4

The temperature remains near normal but the appetite is capricious.

Type B
Produced by the *Feline picornavirus* or *calicivirus*, this causes a rise in temperature to around 104° or 105°F (40° or 40.6°C) and a markedly inflamed or ulcerated pharynx (*photo 6*). There is no coughing or sneezing.

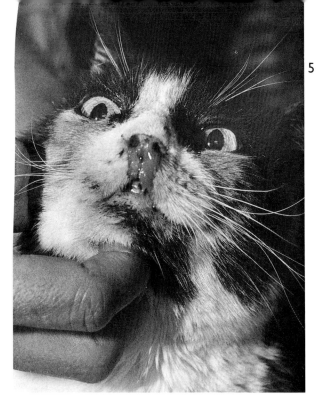

Treatment

5

Both types of so-called cat flu respond rapidly to antibiotic injections, but particularly type B.

Provided I can catch the type B case early enough, a single injection of chloramphenicol combined with long-acting penicillin, cortisone and antihistamine will produce a spectacular cure within 24 hours (*photo 7*). If the cat has been ill for several days, then a second dose may be necessary the following day.

Type A is more difficult to clear and often an initial injection followed by a week's course of oral broad-spectrum antibiotics is required. At the same time, the eyes and nose have to be sponged daily with a piece of cotton wool soaked in warm

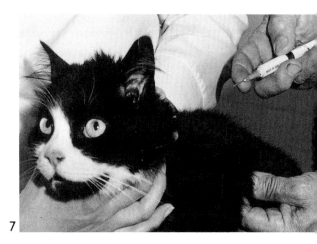

7

water. The eyes often require daily antibiotic drops or ointment.

Considerable success has been obtained by combining broad-spectrum antibiotic therapy with a course of the drug called *chymar*. The recommended dose is ¼ cc daily, by subcutaneous injection, for ten days.

Prevention

A combined vaccine against panleucopaenia, viral rhinotracheitis and *Feline calicivirus* is available.

Feline infectious peritonitis

This is caused by a virus similar to that causing feline leukaemia.

Symptoms

These develop slowly in a chronic form and chiefly appear among young cats under three years,

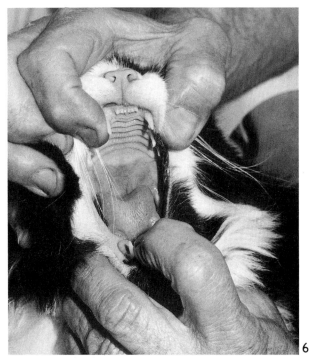

6

The sore throat prevents eating or drinking and, as in panleucopaenia, the patient sits over the drinking bowl as though he wants to drink but can't.

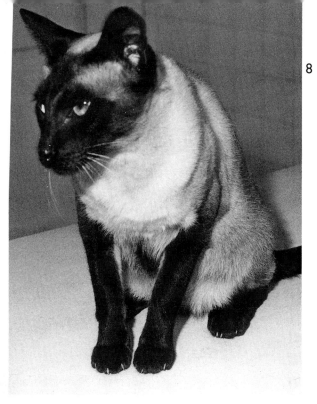

though I have seen the condition in older animals.

There is an initial slight fever (103°F/39.4°C) with a partial loss of appetite and a general depression. The fever subsides but the cat progressively loses condition. It develops anaemia and the abdomen becomes markedly dropsical (*photo 8*).

The illness may last for several months and the membranes often become jaundiced before death.

Treatment

There is no specific treatment and the vast majority of cases die. In fact I have seen only one make an apparent recovery and that remained unthrifty for the rest of its life.

Rabies

This is caused by a virus which attacks all warm-blooded mammals, and it affects the brain.

Method of spread

The virus appears in the saliva of affected animals several days before the symptoms appear and is transmitted mainly by bites although it can enter through a wound. Some cats become infected by eating the carcases of rabies victims.

Symptoms

Symptoms can appear after three weeks, though

8 they sometimes take up to four months to develop. Initially there is a change in the character of the animal. There is a tendency to hide, and the outstanding signs in a rabid cat are excitement and unpredictable viciousness. It will leap at its owner or on other animals and hang on with both teeth and claws.

Within a few days it becomes paralysed, may show convulsions, then goes into a coma and dies.

Treatment

Immediate euthanasia.

Prevention

Vaccination is practised in Europe, Asia, Africa and America. So far we have been able to keep the disease out of the United Kingdom by strict quarantine restrictions. In France it has been discovered that one of the most important factors in preventing spread is the control of foxes.

Vaccination in Britain is permitted only for cats that are being exported to countries where anti-rabies vaccination is compulsory. Your veterinary surgeon will advise on the procedure which involves application to the animal health division of the Ministry of Agriculture, Fisheries and Food.

Rabies is a fatal disease in man and it is absolutely vital that no cat or other warm-blooded pet should be smuggled into this country, so no matter the circumstances never be tempted. In fact it is unwise even to touch a cat when abroad.

Pseudorabies

Pseudorabies or Aujeszky's disease is a rare condition in the cat.

Cause

A virus carried by rats (*photo 9*).

9

Mode of infection
Ingestion of the virus during the killing and/or eating of rats.

Symptoms
Similar to rabies but with one outstanding difference: the cat develops a mad itching of a localised area of its body and it will lick and bite this area raw.

Treatment
There is none.

42
Brain Disorders

Cerebral haemorrhage
I have seen this in older cats.

Cause
Senile arterio-sclerosis (hardening of the arteries).

Symptoms
Not unlike those seen with a middle ear infection. The patient walks round in circles, always in the same direction (*photo 1*). However, with cerebral haemorrhage there is usually partial unilateral paralysis: so that the walk is more of a stagger.

Treatment
Careful nursing is called for, and if there are no further haemorrhages, then recovery is possible.

Meningitis
Inflammation of the meninges, that is, the membranes which surround the brain and spinal cord. It is a very serious condition (*photo 2*).

Cause
Bacteria spreading from an infected wound or abscess.

Symptoms
In the cat I've found in the early stages a high temperature of up to 107°F (41.7°C); other symptoms are a tendency to stagger and fall down and excessive thirst.

If untreated at this stage, fits, often uncontrollable, set in.

Treatment
In the early stage a heavy dose of antibiotic may produce a spectacular improvement. Once the fits start, the condition is hopeless and euthanasia is indicated.

1

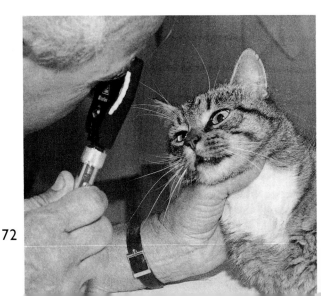

43
Toxoplasmosis

This is caused by a protozoan parasite called the *Toxoplasma gondii*, whose natural host is the cat.

It has recently been established by research workers that the cat is the only animal that excretes the toxoplasma parasite in its faeces. Contamination of food by these faeces is the dangerous source of toxoplasmosis in sheep. And humans, of course, are in danger if they handle faecal-stained cat fur.

Symptoms

In a young cat the *Toxoplasma gondii* causes an acute pneumonia. In older cats it produces brain symptoms — staggering and loss of balance (*photo 1*).

Treatment

There is no specific treatment, and since the disease can be transmitted to humans, euthanasia should always be considered. See Zoonoses.

1

44
Anaemia

Feline infectious anaemia

This is caused by a blood parasite called *Eperythrozoon felis* (also known as *Haemobartonella felis*), which attacks the red blood corpuscles.

Many cats carry this parasite without ever showing adverse symptoms.

A flare-up happens only when the cat's natural resistance is markedly lowered by stress, starvation or disease.

Symptoms

A high persistent fever ($104° - 105°F/ 40° - 40.6°C$) with loss of appetite and rapidly developing acute anaemia. The cat becomes acutely depressed and weak.

Treatment

This should be left entirely to your veterinary surgeon. He will prescribe antibiotics, iron and vitamin B_{12} (*photo 1*).

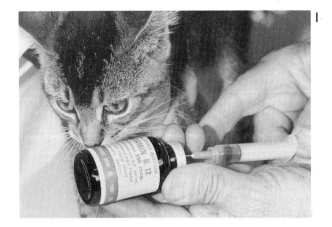

Other causes of anaemia

1. Excess bleeding from a wound
2. Heavy infestation of fleas or lice which suck blood
3. Rat poison (warfarin), which not only damages the blood vessels but prevents any escaping blood from clotting
4. Other poisons such as lead and phenol
5. Bacterial toxins
6. Such drugs as phenacetin and sulphafurazole; aspirin; insecticides; the antibiotic chloramphenicol
7. Damage to the bone marrow by direct injury.

45
Diabetes

In my experience this is not common in the cat but it does occur.

There are two types:

Diabetes mellitus, which is caused by a deficiency of the pancreatic secretion insulin which controls the carbohydrate metabolism. This can be triggered off by excessive dosing with cortisone.

Diabetes insipidus, which is caused by a shortage of an anti-diuretic hormone normally secreted by the pituitary gland at the base of the brain.

Diabetes mellitus

Seen mainly in older neutered cats and more commonly in warm climates.

Symptoms

Excessive drinking and passage of urine. Loss of flesh and energy.

If untreated, emaciation is progressive and the mouth is foul with tartar deposits. Cataracts develop in the lens of the eye.

Treatment

Consult your veterinary surgeon as early as possible. He will confirm the diagnosis by examining the urine or blood, and will prescribe daily subcutaneous injections of 5 to 10 units of protamine zinc insulin (*photo 1*).

Overdosing with insulin may cause weakness, staggering or coma. If any of these signs appear, give the cat 2 or 3 teaspoonfuls of honey, syrup or glucose and get it to a veterinary surgeon quickly.

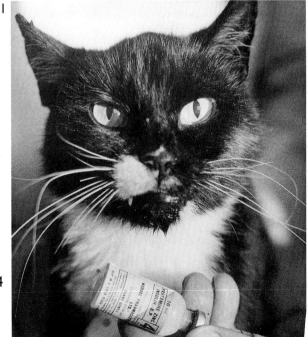

Dietetical changes are not necessary, but any infection the patient may pick up will have to be treated immediately because *Diabetes mellitus* makes the cat susceptible to bacteria.

Diabetes insipidus
Rarely seen in the cat.

Symptoms
Excessive drinking and passing large volumes of watery urine.

Treatment
Intramuscular injection of a hormone called pitressin repeated every third day.

46
Poisoning

Pasteurellosis
Cause
A germ called *Pasteurella pseudo-tuberculosis*.

Source
Infected rodents and birds (*photo 1*).

Symptoms
Sudden onset of acute gastro-enteritis with intense thirst and emaciation.

In the more chronic types diarrhoea is the main symptom and this may alternate with constipation.

Treatment
Tranquillisers to control the vomiting and a five-day course of broad-spectrum antibiotic given orally. The pasteurella bug can affect humans.

Salmonellosis
Cause
Three species of the salmonella germ: *Salmonella enteritidis*, *Salmonella typhimurium* and *Salmonella cholerae-suis*.

Source
Infected rats and mice (*photo 2*). Kittens may occasionally pick up the bug from infected food.

Symptoms
More or less identical to those of pasteurellosis.

Treatment
As for pasteurellosis. The veterinary surgeon will probably swab the faeces for laboratory examination to determine the germ involved.

Botulism
Cause
The germ called the *Clostridium botulinum*. Fortunately this very severe form of food poisoning is rare since the smell of the infected meat makes it unpalatable to the cat.

Steatitis
This is a condition where there occurs a yellow or bright orange discolouration of fat, especially under the skin of the belly (*photo 3*).

3 **Cause**
Excess diet of fish scraps or tinned fish.

Symptoms
Are those of a hepatitis (inflammation of the liver), namely, listlessness and abdominal tenderness, followed by acute jaundice. The patient shows a reluctance to move.

Treatment
Vitamin E and vitamin B injections together with vitamin E tablets (tocopheral) given by mouth.

Unusual poisons
Common human medicines
Vegetable laxative tablets (BPC) cause severe diarrhoea and continuous vomiting.

Less than half an aspirin tablet will cause toxic symptoms of nausea and vomiting.

Anti-depressant drugs (tranquillisers) can also be a problem.

Other poisons
The four most dangerous poisons are lead (picked up as old paint flakes), strychnine (got from the bones of birds and rodents poisoned by gamekeepers), warfarin (rat poison) and the organophosphorus compounds used in insecticidal sprays (*colour plate 22*).

Treatment
Your veterinary surgeon can successfully treat all these provided he sees the cases early enough. Strychnine patients have to be heavily sedated for several days.

47
The Key-Gaskell Syndrome

Cause
Unknown, but the condition does not appear to be highly contagious, a fact which would lead one to suspect some type of poisoning. The incubation period is anything from ten to twelve hours to

several days. It affects all ages of all breeds of both sexes.

Symptoms
The pupils of both eyes are usually markedly dilated

(hence the alternative name of dilated pupil syndrome) and do not contract in bright light (*photo 1 and colour plate 23*); sometimes only one eye is affected. The cat goes off its food and when it tries to eat appears to chew and swallow with considerable difficulty, often grinding its teeth in the process.

Vomiting and general depression produces a dry nose and mouth and protrusion of the third eyelid across part of the eye.

Perhaps the most persistent sign is constipation with an occasional history of an initial diarrhoea. In severe cases, as the condition progresses, the cat becomes weak and debilitated and may have difficulty in passing urine.

Treatment
Since the cause is not as yet known, treatment is aimed at alleviating the symptoms, and of course such treatment must be under the direct supervision of a veterinary surgeon. He will give intravenous or subcutaneous fluids to combat the dehydration and may recommend the force feeding of fluids such as complan, glucose and water and meat essence.

He will prescribe pilocarpine eye drops to contract the pupils and increase the flow of saliva, plus twice daily dosing with a drug with the proprietary name of Myotonine which helps to

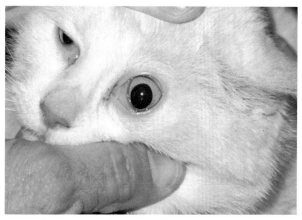

control vomiting, improve the dry nose and mouth, ease the constipation and prevent bladder paralysis.

If secondary symptoms occur, the veterinary surgeon may have to prescribe antibiotics and/or steroids.

Prognosis
The prognosis is not good, as the overall mortality rate is between 70 and 80 per cent. The fortunate cats that do recover may have to be treated for up to a year before the eyes and digestive system return to normal.

In my experience cats that keep trying to eat have the best chance of surviving.

48
Bone Disorders

Feline juvenile osteodystrophy
Cause
Dietetical deficiency of calcium, e.g., kittens fed exclusively on minced beef or sheep's heart may develop the disease within two months.

Symptoms
The kitten becomes less active and may suffer

from bent legs and greenstick fractures (*photo 1*).

Treatment and prevention
Access to cow's milk during the growing period is usually all that is necessary. Cow's milk contains sufficient calcium for the kitten's needs and will balance the intake of protein from the meat. Since most kittens have access to milk or cream, osteodystrophy is not often seen.

1

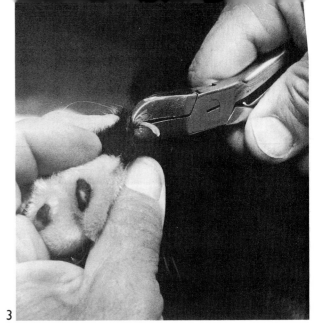

3

Fractures

These are many and varied but should always be left to your veterinary surgeon to diagnose and treat (*photo 2*).

X-rays are readily available in the majority of veterinary clinics, and the results of orthopaedic surgery are often spectacularly successful. Surgical techniques, in many cases identical to those used in humans, ensure that your pet has the maximum chance of recovery.

Pelvic fractures

These are commonly seen after road accidents.

In the cat, the prognosis is often excellent, treatment comprising merely a restriction of movement for a month after a few days of sedation to combat pain.

Broken claws

Occasionally seen after fighting.

The veterinary surgeon will remove the claw under local or general anaesthesia (*photo 3*).

Removal of claws

In many countries declawing (onchectomy) is practised fairly frequently, but the operation is generally frowned on in Britain despite the fact that it can be done painlessly.

2

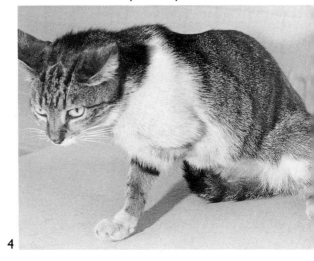

4

Fracture of the jaw

This is very common. Usually the veterinary surgeon can wire the fracture satisfactorily.

Amputation

This means the removal of the whole or part of a limb or tail, and the procedure is advisable if the part is irreparably damaged or infected.

In the cat, amputation can be embarked upon with complete confidence, since the ability of the cat to adapt itself to the loss of a limb is quite remarkable (*photo 4*).

Modern anaesthesia and surgery make the operation painless and safe.

Dislocations

The commonest sites of dislocation in the cat are the hip joints, the elbow (*photo 5*) and the jaw.

Immediate veterinary attention is indicated, since the quicker the dislocation is reduced, the better the chance of complete recovery. Not only so, but dislocations are extremely painful.

In all cases veterinary surgeons will use general anaesthesia.

Bone tumours — neoplasms

A cancer, usually an osteosarcoma, is not infrequently seen in the bones of a cat. If a leg bone is affected, amputation may give the cat a few extra years of happy life, but in all cases the diagnosis and decision should be left to your veterinary surgeon. Three types of bone cancer can occur.

Osteomyelitis

Means an inflammation of the bone marrow. It may flare up secondary to an injury.

Diagnosis and treatment is the strict province of a veterinary surgeon. If antibiotic therapy is not successful, amputation may be necessary.

Radial paralysis

Paralysis of the radial nerve which passes over the front of the shoulder and controls the muscles that normally extend the limb.

Cause

Injury by a blow or accident.

Symptoms

The cat carries the leg with the knee and fetlock bent forward.

Treatment

Patience and time. If the front of the fetlock is dragging on the ground, it may be necessary to amputate the leg.

Arthritis

Inflammation of the surface of a joint (*colour plate 24*). It is uncommon in cats but occasionally seen in advancing years.

Treatment

Considerable relief can be given by modern drugs prescribed by your veterinary surgeon.

5

49
Zoonoses

This rather mysterious word simply means diseases that can spread from animals to man. Clients often ask if they can catch catarrh from their snuffling cat. The simple answer is no, though there are other cat infections that humans can get. Fortunately these are comparatively few, and there are none that cannot be prevented by commonsense, hygiene and cat care.

Fleas, mites, ringworm, tapeworm and the larvae of the roundworm *Toxocara cati* can all occasionally cause trouble, especially in children.

However with proper veterinary care and routine handwashing after handling, the risks are almost negligible.

In countries where rabies is present cats are an ever-present possible source of that killer disease, but in Britain the only serious potential danger is toxoplasmosis (see page 73). *Toxoplasma gondii* can cause abortion and foetal abnormalities in pregnant women. For this reason it is advisable for pregnant women to avoid handling cats or at least to wash their hands thoroughly after doing so.

50
Homoeopathy for Cats

There seems little doubt that homoeopathy has a place in the treatment of selected cat ailments.

Homoeopathy is the medical practice of treating an illness with a substance that produces the same symptoms as the illness. In other words, it concentrates on treating the patient rather than on treating the disease.

Several veterinary surgeons specialise in this type of therapy often combining it with traditional treatments. Obviously it must be left to the individual veterinary surgeon to recommend homoeopathy if or when he thinks it is indicated.

51
Accidents and Minor Ailments

The most common accidents are:
   Car accidents
   Dangerous liquids on the coat
   Burns

Road accidents
It has often been said that a cat has nine lives. I've seen this apparently borne out again and again with cats that have been hit on the road.

If the wheel of the vehicle has not passed over the chest or abdomen, the power of the cat to survive is incredible.

Recommended procedure
In all cases of injury on the road, lift the cat as carefully as possible with the palms of both hands, one under the shoulders and one under the hind-quarters. Place the cat on the car seat on its side, cover it over with a rug or blanket and drive to a veterinary surgeon as quickly as possible.

Never attempt any first-aid treatment, other than applying a tourniquet to a limb if it is bleeding excessively.

Liquids on the coat
The usual contaminants are oil, tar, paraffin, creosote and paint (*photo 1*).

Don't delay treatment because the cat will try to lick the contaminant and then you'll have burns in the mouth to contend with. Also, the skin of a cat rapidly absorbs poisonous liquids to produce dangerous and often fatal systemic poisoning.

Recommended procedure
Prepare a bath by half-filling the sink with warm water. Add a generous helping of ordinary washing up liquid detergent.

With an assistant to hold the patient by the scruff of the neck, immerse the body of the cat in the bath and gently and patiently cleanse the coat (*photo 2*).

After the bath, dry the cat thoroughly, then take along to the veterinary surgeon who will prescribe an oral antidote in case any of the poisonous liquid has been absorbed or swallowed, e.g., the antidote to tar and creosote poisoning is Epsom salts.

With paint, clip off all contaminated fur.

Burns
The cat looking for affection or food at lunchtime often places itself in a vulnerable position to be scalded by boiling water from the cooking pots.

Recommended procedure
An immediate visit to the veterinary surgeon. The thick fur often hides the extent of the injury.

The veterinary surgeon will clip the hair and apply antibiotic cream containing anti-inflammatory

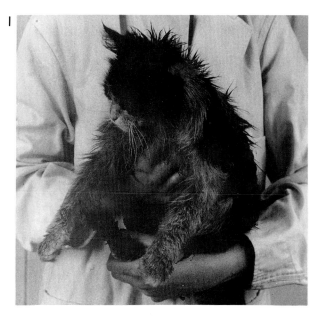

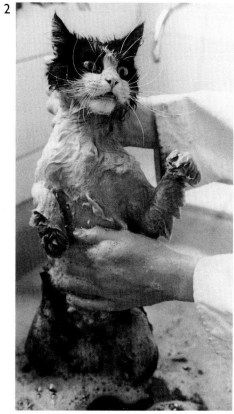

drugs which will remove the pain rapidly (*photo 3*).

Neglect may lead to large areas of the back skin scaling and sloughing off, leaving granulating wounds that will take months to heal.

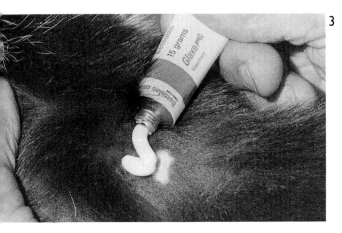
3

Cause

The germ called the *Clostridium tetani* which grows and multiplies in deep punctured wounds. During its growth the germ excretes toxins which travel along the nerves to the spinal column.

Symptoms

The third eyelid (the membrana nictitans) may cover most of the eye and the cat may walk stiffly, the muscles of the limbs and/or back being tightly contracted. Any sudden noise will provoke painful spasms. The jaw may or may not be locked.

Treatment

A suspect cat should be placed in a quiet dark room until a veterinary surgeon arrives. He will inject penicillin and tetanus antitoxin together with sedatives and muscle relaxants. If the jaw is not locked, there is a reasonable chance that treatment may prove successful.

Scratches and bites

Few household pets go through life without being attacked by other cats or by dogs and without being bitten by a rodent.

Recommended procedure

If you see a scratch or bite wound on your pet (*photo 4*), take it along to the veterinary surgeon. All cat wounds are highly susceptible to infection and a single injection of long-acting antibiotic will often prevent an abscess formation.

Never apply an antiseptic to the wound, especially **iodine**, since the application will be rapidly absorbed and may cause poisoning.

Abscesses

Probably the most frequent minor ailment veterinary surgeons have to treat is an abscess on the cat's leg, head, neck (*photo 5*) or body (*colour plate 25*). Such abscesses result from unseen or neglected scratch or bite wounds, especially rat bites.

Recommended procedure

Don't just bathe the abscess and allow it to burst on its own. If you do, it will reform within two or three weeks.

Let your veterinary surgeon deal with it. He will open the abscess right up using local or general anaesthesia, drain it thoroughly (*photo 6*), and fill the cavity with long-acting antibiotic. At the same time he will inject the patient with a large dose of long-acting antibiotic to prevent the abscess reforming.

Tetanus

This is a rare condition in the cat but it can occur, though in fifty years of veterinary practice I have seen only one case.

4

5

Stings

By bees, wasps and other insects.

Recommended procedure

Although a minor summer ailment, a sting, especially in the head region, can cause severe respiratory distress. So a quick visit to the veterinary surgeon is well worthwhile. He will inject the cat with antihistamine and antibiotic and recovery will be rapid.

If the wasp sting is visible, it can be removed with eyebrow tweezers but this is no easy job with a struggling cat.

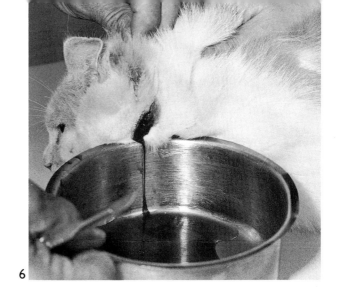

6

Heat exhaustion and sunstroke

This can occur when the cat is locked up in a car or cupboard, or if forced to lie in direct sunlight in a restricted area, or when confined to an excessively hot and humid cage in a cattery.

Recommended procedure

The symptoms are complete prostration and a rise in temperature of up to five degrees. Breathing is distressed.

The best first-aid remedy is to plunge the cat into a cold bath three or four times in rapid succession, then place it in the coolest spot available. If this fails, take it to a veterinary surgeon immediately.

7

Constipation

Fairly common minor ailment in the household cat.

Recommended procedure

Add a teaspoonful of liquid paraffin to each feed, mashing it in well to avoid detection. Alternately feed some sardines in olive oil (*photo 7*).

If the constipation persists more than two days, then consult your veterinary surgeon.

Diarrhoea

Most cases of mild diarrhoea in an otherwise healthy cat can be cleared up by withholding food for twelve hours, then mixing half a level teaspoonful of kaolin powder into the feed.

If, however, the diarrhoea persists for over forty-eight hours, a visit to the vet is indicated. If possible, take a sample of the stool with you.

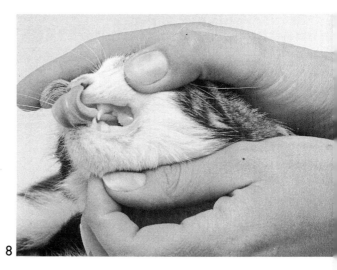

8

Facial paralysis

Facial paralysis occurs when there is damage to the facial nerve which passes behind each ear and ramifies down both sides of the face.

Cause

Pressure on the nerve by a brain tumour inside the skull or external damage to the nerve by wounds or abscesses (*colour plate 26*).

Symptoms

As the name suggests, one side of the face is paralysed with the affected lip hanging down (*photo 8*); sometimes saliva runs from the paralysed corner of the mouth.

Treatment

If the paralysis is secondary to a wound or abscess, then patience is needed. Time and time only will heal the nerve and correct the deformity.

If due to a brain tumour, euthanasia is indicated.

52
Emergencies

Apart from the accidents already described, several other emergencies may occur, e.g., electric shock, shock, drowning, prolapse, poisoning and fits. Another occasional emergency can be caused by an elastic band.

Electric shock

Seen usually when the kitten or cat has been chewing a live flex (*photo 1*). The patient will probably be stuck to the source of the electric current.

Recommended procedure

Never attempt to pull the cat away from the flex with your bare hands; if you do you will probably join it on the floor.

Even after switching off the current, cover your hand with a rubber glove or an old rubber boot and gently pull the cat clear. Then drive the patient to the nearest veterinary surgeon as quickly as possible.

If a veterinary surgeon is not available immediately, then apply artificial respiration.

Lay the cat on its side on a table. Extend the neck, pull the tongue out and fix it between the teeth.

Place the flat of the hand on the ribs and press down firmly but not viciously. You will hear the air being expelled from the lungs; when this happens remove your hand from the chest and let the lungs expand. Repeat the process every two seconds

84

until the cat moves its tongue or starts to breathe of its own accord.

Whatever you do, never attempt to give a shocked or unconscious cat brandy or any other stimulant. If you do you'll choke it.

Shock
A condition where there is a sudden fall in blood pressure with a consequent oxygen deficiency and a drop in body temperature.

Cause
Usually a road accident with or without internal or external haemorrhage.

Major surgical operations involving loss of body tissues or excess of fluids can also cause shock as can the fatigue and exhaustion of prolonged labour during kitting.

Symptoms
Inability to stand; ice-cold pallid mucous membranes, in the mouth and eyes particularly.

The pulse is weak and rapid and the breathing often shallow.

Treatment
Get your injured cat to a veterinary surgeon as quickly as possible — successful treatment depends on speed of application.

As a first-aid measure wrap the patient in a warm blanket **but do not use a hot water bottle, and never try to give brandy or any other fluid**.

Drowning
Cats are excellent swimmers and will only drown if unable to climb out of a tank or if rough water makes them swallow excess.

Recommended procedure
Grab the cat firmly by the scruff of the neck and lift it out of the water. Then grip the hind legs above the hocks and swing the cat round in a wide circle several times (*photo 2*). This will clear the mouth and windpipe of water and mucus.

Now place the cat on a flat table and apply artificial respiration. At the same time get someone to phone for the veterinary surgeon.

Prolapse
Two types occur in the cat: rectal and uterine.

2

RECTAL PROLAPSE

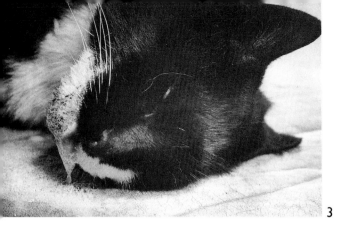

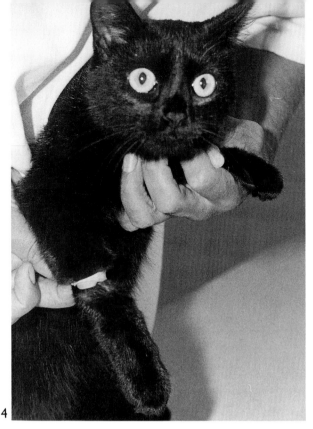

3

Rectal prolapse

Seen mainly in kittens suffering from diarrhoea. The repeated straining causes the rectum to prolapse like the finger of a glove being turned inside out (*see diagram*).

Recommended procedure

An immediate visit to the veterinary surgeon. He will anaesthetise the kitten, replace the prolapse and suture the anal ring, treat the kitten for shock and prescribe a cure for the diarrhoea.

Uterine prolapse

This is seen only in queens after the birth of the kittens.

Recommended procedure

Place the kittens on a blanket in a cardboard box and put them in the oven (NB: *not* a microwave) at a temperature of around 80°F (26.7°C), then rush the queen to the veterinary clinic.

The veterinary surgeon will operate at once. He will replace the uterus under a general anaesthetic and treat the patient for shock. If the queen is required for further breeding, he will fix the uterine horns with catgut sutures to the abdominal wall. If no further breeding is planned, he will probably do an ovario-hysterectomy.

Fits

Fortunately fits in the cat are not common. During a fit the cat loses consciousness and froths at the mouth (*photo 3*) but is not in any pain, though the sight is very distressing to the owner.

Recommended procedure

Place the cat on a bed of newspapers on the floor of the bathroom and leave it to recover on its own. When it does, consult your veterinary surgeon.

Fits are due to some form of brain damage and

4

can be caused by any of the following:

    Concussion
    Certain poisons (e.g. strychnine)
    Encephalitis (inflammation of the brain secondary to infection)
    Epilepsy (rare in the cat)
    Obviously the diagnosis and treatment of fits is very much a job for a veterinary surgeon.

One of the signs of brain damage is nystagmus, a side-to-side flicking of the eyes.

Elastic bands

Occasionally a cat's paw, leg or neck region will swell up alarmingly. Such cases are often caused by elastic bands placed there by unthinking, forgetful children (*photo 4*).

A quick visit to the veterinary surgeon will solve the problem, though he may have to anaesthetise the cat to dig out the band.

Euthanasia

Euthanasia means painless putting to sleep. All veterinary surgeons have the perfect method immediately available.

On no account should you ever attempt to drown a cat or kittens — such a procedure is not only against the law but it is cruel and barbaric.

Index

Farming Press Books

Listed below are a number of the agricultural and veterinary books published by Farming Press. For more information or a free illustrated book list please contact:

**Farming Press Books, 4 Friars Courtyard
30-32 Princes Street, Ipswich IPI IRJ, United Kingdom
Telephone (0473) 241122**

Dog Ailments   Eddie Straiton

The diagnosis and treatment of common dog ailments shown with 400 photographs and a clear text

Good Dog   Jack Howell

How to train a dog in general obedience, tracking, searching, work against criminals, and for demonstration purposes

The Blue Riband of the Heather   E B Carpenter

A pictorial cavalcade showing all the Supreme Champions of the International Sheep Dog Trials from 1906 to 1989

A Way of Life   Glyn Jones and Barbara Collins

The techniques of sheepdog handling, training and trialling explained by an International Supreme Championship trialist

The Showman Shepherd   David Turner

How to show sheep: housing, feeding, grading and finishing, trimming, halter training, preparation of specific breeds, ringmanship

TV Vet Horse Book   Eddie Straiton

Recognition and treatment of common horse and pony ailments

Farming Press Books is part of the Morgan-Grampian Farming Press group which publishes a range of farming magazines: Arable Farming, Dairy Farmer, Farming News, Livestock Farming, Pig Farming, What's New in Farming. *For a specimen copy of any of these please contact the address above.*